Loving and Leaving
the
Good Life

Loving and Leaving the Good Life

the

Good Life

HELEN NEARING

CHELSEA GREEN PUBLISHING COMPANY
POST MILLS, VERMONT

"Unforgotten" is reprinted by permission of
The Putnam Publishing Group from *The Spell of
the Yukon* by Robert Service. Copyright © 1907, 1916 by
Dodd, Mead & Company, Inc. Used by permission of the
Estate of Robert Service. Excerpt from "The Wind Bloweth
Where It Listeth" is reprinted by permission of GRM Associates,
Inc., Agents for the Estate of Ida M. Cullen from the book *Copper
Sun* by Countee Cullen. Copyright © 1927 by Harper &
Brothers, renewed by Ida M. Cullen. Excerpts from *The
Poems of W. B. Yeats: A New Edition*, edited by Richard J.
Finneran, are reprinted by permission of Macmillan
Publishing Company. Copyright © 1928 by
Macmillan Publishing Company, renewed
1956 by Georgie Yeats.

Library of Congress Cataloging-in-Publication Data
Nearing, Helen
Loving and leaving the good life / Helen Nearing.
p. cm.
ISBN 0–930031–63–6
1. Nearing, Helen, 1904– 2. Nearing, Scott, 1883–1983.
3. Country life—New England. 4. New England—
Biography. I. title.
S521.N34   1992   335' .0092—dc20   91–44013
[B]   CIP

Contents

There is no thing that dying, dies forever:
Nothing is so forespent
But it may somehow finally recapture
That first content,
Wrought of the frail and protoplasmic splendor
Of element.

There is no song, once sung, made still forever:
Never such hush profound
But somewhere in the fibers of creation
Under the ground
And over the light of stars in the summer heavens
Makes cosmic sound.

There is no love, once told, that dies completely:
Never such love has grown
But scatters seed producing in its likeness
From zone to zone:
Shaping the destiny of men and angels
In worlds unknown.

poet unknown

No Longer the Two of Us

How will you manage
To cross alone
The autumn mountain
Which was so hard to get across
Even when we went the two of us together?

Chinese, Seventh Century

*W*HEN ONE DOOR CLOSES, another opens . . .
into another room, another space, other happenings. There are
many doors to open and close in our lives. Some doors we
leave ajar, where we hope and plan to return. Some doors are
slammed shut decisively—"No more of *that!*" Some are closed
regretfully, softly—"It was good, but it is over." Departures en-
tail arrivals somewhere else. Closing a door, leaving it behind,
means opening onto new vistas and ventures, new possibilities,
new incentives.

My life was not over and done with, though a chapter
ended, when Scott, comrade and love of fifty-three years, quietly breathed away his life at home in Maine three weeks after
his hundredth birthday. He went with dignity, purposefully fasting, after a long and a good life. I had to pick up the reins that
had of late been held, though loosely, in his hands.

With Scott gone, I chose to live by myself. I was not lonely;
I enjoyed the quiet and solitude, and almost resented the constant calls and visits of solicitous friends. I did not need them. I
preferred to be alone if I could not go on living with Scott.

There were many things still to be done. What was to become of the woodland house we had lived in on the banks of Penobscot Bay? Forest Farm was still visited by pilgrims who wanted to see the stone house we had built in our seventies and nineties, the stone-walled garden and greenhouse, and our extensive library. I still entertained almost as many visitors as we had had when Scott was alive and participating. I continued to keep the place as a Good Life Center where people could come to see the wide-ranging files he had kept and the numerous scrapbooks of photographs and letters I had collected after his last birthday and his death day. Here they could obtain his books and sometimes even help maintain the grounds. He would have wanted an open house, not a memorial museum. That is how I would try to keep it as long as I lived.

I rhymed, in a jingle, a release to him and to the house we had built.

> Who will reap what we have built here,
> In this house and on this land?
> You and I will be forgotten
> But our work and house will stand.
> Other folk will come and go here;
> Others take their places, too.
> We will leave our blessing for them:
> Happiness in what they do.

I could manage on my own. I knew I mustn't mope. I remembered an ancient Chinese saying: "We cannot help the birds of sadness flying over our heads, but we need not let them build nests in our hair." I would try to live as though Scott were still here. He had been a treasure-house of help in the home. There had been a great sense of security with him around. Now I found myself alone and had to cope with all and everybody.

"Of all mortal beings," wrote Samuel Johnson in a 1780 letter of sympathy to a friend who had lost his wife, ". . . one must lose the other. He that outlives a wife whom he has long loved, sees himself disjoined from the only mind that had the same hopes and fears and interests; from the only companion with whom he has shared much good or evil; with whom he could set his mind at liberty, to retrace the past or anticipate the future. The continuity of being is lacerated, the settled course of sentiment is stopped; life stands suspended and motionless, till it is driven by external causes into a new channel. But the time of suspense is dreadful."

My first few months after Scott's passing were a blessed blank in my mind. Friends say I tended to all the usual activities with regularity and apparent cheer, but that there was a distance and a numbness which they sensed. I responded to those who came, but proffered little of myself.

C. S. Lewis has written in *A Grief Observed*: "Bereavement is a universal and integral part of our experience of love. It follows marriage as normally as marriage follows courtship or as autumn follows summer. It is not a truncation of the process but one of the phases; not the interruption of the dance, but the next figure. We are taken out of ourselves by the loved one when he is here. Then comes the tragic figure of the dance in which we must learn to be still taken out of ourselves though the bodily presence is withdrawn."

I had always known that Scott, twenty-one years older than I, would very likely go first, but I rarely thought about it. He was so strong, so vital, so charged with life; surely he would always be there. I never envisioned him off the scene. But now it had come and he was gone from sight and sound; no more to work daily in the garden, to toss seaweed into our truck. No more reading aloud together in the evenings by the fireplace; no more trips together around the world; no more books from his pen or cogent comments on world events. He had gone out of our harmonious unity a little ahead of me.

I was given extra time to clear things up, make the right decisions and arrangements for the house, our books and papers, the garden, and then go on myself. I was ready to leave any minute. In fact, the going could not come too quickly. I had had an extraordinarily good life, but was becoming increasingly detached from the details of everyday things. If there had been a shining sea to sink into, I would have gladly relinquished my body to be part of the all. On the other hand, if there was more work to be done when one got over there, I was ready to face that with, please, a little interim between to catch breath and look around.

I saw that the key to my further life was in my own hands. I now knew that when we choose to go we can go at any time, nonviolently, calmly and tranquilly, dying with dignity. We can stop eating, as Scott had done. If death is our aim, then food is our bane, the lure that keeps us tied to the body. Stop feeding your creature body and it declines and dies. Death is not the ending of the adventure of life. It is merely the end of the body.

Gandhi wrote in a letter to a disciple: "The more I observe and study things, the more convinced I become that sorrow over separation is perhaps the greatest delusion. To realize that it is a delusion is to become free. We love friends for the substance we recognize in them and yet deplore the destruction of the insubstantial that covers the substance for the time being. There is no death, no separation for the substance. Real friendship touches and can keep the substance when the surface goes."

A profound thought on life and death is recorded from Apolonius of Tyana in the first century A.D.: "There is no death of anything save in appearance. That which passes over from essence to nature seems to be birth, and what passes over from nature to essence seems to be death. Nothing really is originated, and nothing ever perishes, but only now comes into sight and now vanishes."

Scott once wrote to a friend who queried him on what he thought of the possibility of life after death. "I prefer to put the question differently: Does a man go on keeping company with the universe of which he is a part? I have come to the conclusion that life goes on for a substantial range of experiences which differ a great deal. Life is not simple, but complex, and one of its complexities is the division of life into fragments of longer or shorter duration, but certainly more durable than the apparatus with which we pursue the life on this earth."

There is too much "I" in our lives. The personality is not our inner core but something that we wear. We are not our bodies; we are that which uses our bodies. We are not our thoughts; we are that which directs our thought. We are not our emotions; we are that which feels our emotions. We play roles with our personalities that may be worthwhile or deplorable, that can make or mar the world.

The universe is too magnificent as it rolls on to concern itself overmuch with personalities. The greatest thing we can do with our lives is to realize and live in the entirety rather than in our own puny selves.

I remember an episode forty or more years ago when a group of friends was seated around a kitchen table in southern Vermont. A midday meal was going on, with a good deal of talk from a visitor, a distinguished woman who was telling of her peace work around the world. I was disturbed by the constant use of the first person pronoun in her conversation. I ventured a suggestion.

"How possible would it be to go through the whole day, or even an hour, or a meal such as this, without using the word 'I'?" The rest of the company agreed it would be an interesting experiment. We decided to try it then and there.

The room became silent while possible approaches to the problem were considered. There were long pauses and involved reconstructions of sentences before even a simple idea was risked. The "I" intruded continually and often had to be rebuffed or shouted down. Many fresh starts were made and it was difficult for us to carry on anything like a spontaneous conversation.

"This is ridiculous! We'll never get anywhere this way," said our noted guest finally, refusing to go on with what she called just a game. We all learned, I hope, from the memorable meal how self-oriented we are in everyday speech—just how much "I" there is in our lives. Try it sometime and see for yourself if and for how long you can manage to eliminate the first person from your talk. You will tend to become mute. Not such a bad thing.

What and who is this "I" anyway? We call the body "mine." We inhabit it; yet it is not us. What and who is this "I" that we aggrandize and center upon all through our lives? We are all part of the same unity—life. The only reality is the oneness, yet the self-sense is paramount in most people, ignored or bypassed only by a few. Can we become less self-centered? How far can we eliminate the ego in our cosmos?

Here I find myself confronted by exactly this problem. What can be done by the author of a memoir to avoid contaminating the pages with too many first-person pronouns? Can this story of living and learning and loving and leaving the good life be written without the continual cavalcade of "I," "I," "I" cavorting throughout? Can the first person singular be pushed into the background?

Jiddu Krishnamurti, the Indian philosopher and public speaker, adopted a phrase in his later talks which was admirably impersonal. Instead of using "I" when mentioning himself or his own experiences, he said "the speaker" did this or "the speaker" thought that.

Scott used the word "I" rarely in his books or lectures, and even as little as possible in his everyday conversation, which he kept to a minimum and which was curiously communal throughout. He was not a self-centered person. He always said "our pond," not the pond he dug and carted off in thousands of wheelbarrows of soil for the garden. Although he planted and cultivated most of it, he always called it "our garden." It was "Helen's house," not his or even ours, though he toiled in the building of it as much as I did. I like to live in the company of such people who think beyond the self.

Neither Scott nor I have ever written in our books about our inner lives. Both of us preferred to be reserved and private people, though we came much into the public eye. It was hard for him to write his autobiography. He thought it too egocentric and was only persuaded to do so by having pointed out to him the historical aspects of the life he had lived, through a century of great change. He wrote the book as a political autobiography. I got an incidental half-dozen lines, which tickled me immensely.

In dedicating this book to Scott and binding it around his memory, I must outline the part of my life that came before we met. A few of those years were lived in connection with Krishnamurti, so that should also enter into the story. But the book is Scott-centered, as my life for more than fifty years was Scott-centered. There was only one sun in my life. Krishnamurti entered it as might a comet and left it as suddenly, soon disappearing from my sight. He dazzled my eyes in my teens, but this proved to be but an interlude.

Life is a great network of possibilities consisting of grasped opportunities and of pitfalls for all participants. Every entity, every act, is part of the great manifestation. Every living thing adds its note, its song, its contribution through every moment of its existence. As we live our lives we leave our mark. Whatever the world may be like a hundred years from now, it will be influenced in part by what each one of us has been, has done and thought. So the marks that my parents, my brother and sister, my longtime love and husband, Scott Nearing, and I myself have made together and separately have helped shape the world, have influenced others' lives, and the lives of you who may read these pages.

I wrote this story originally in the third person, as more decent and impersonal. Able editors advised a "me" and "I" account as essential to give contact and the human touch. I tried their way but felt uncomfortable and presumptuous. Every "I" set down offended me. I dislike the eternal "I" and would happily go through life (and this book) without it. So, against expert advice, I persisted in telling the story of Helen and Scott from the distance of "she" and "he" and "they." Then, to counter continued disapproval, I tried a mixture—a rocking back and forth from the first gear to third, shifting when I couldn't stand the "I" any longer.

So here, dear reader, after all my earlier protestations about the paltriness of personalities, is a book about "us," "we," "me." If I sometimes in desperation or aversion use the "she" and "they," slipping into third gear for a while, you will understand and bear with me?

Here, then, is presented an opened window into my brief contact with Krishnamurti, but mainly into my relationship with Scott Nearing and our similar outlook on life. It is not, as in the other books Scott and I have written together, a report on our physical and mental work together, our homesteading, our diet, gardening, or building operations. Here is an effort to share more of our half century of living and loving the good life and our various leavings and startings over.

There really should be a comma after the first word in the title of this book. It is not only loving the good life that is meant, but loving, as a specific and essential ingredient of the good life.

When We Two Met

*Of more than common friendliness
When first we met we did not guess.*

Robert Bridges, "Triolet (16)," 1873

I WAS a seventeen-year-old schoolgirl when I was taken by a teacher to an adult gathering at Scott Nearing's home in Ridgewood, New Jersey. The political conversation was above my head and I sat beside the fireplace wondering why I had been dragged there. I was the only young person present. That was my first and, as far as I then knew it to be, my last contact with Scott Nearing.

A chance telephone call made years later, when I was twenty-four, initiated our second meeting. At my father's request (and how he later regretted it) I called Scott Nearing asking him to speak at a local club of which my father was president. He remembered the observant girl who had taken no part in the general conversation so many years before.

After agreeing to talk for a Unitarian Church forum, he asked me what I had been doing in the intervening years. I told him of my years studying the violin in Europe, of my travels in India and my time in Australia. We spoke for a while on the telephone. I liked his voice; it was warm and strong and friendly. Something must have drawn him too, for later in the week he called and asked me to drive with him on an errand to upstate New York where we could enjoy the brilliant autumn coloring together. Just for the sound of his voice, I broke an outstanding date with a new young man to go with Scott. That weekend started it all.

In our drive upstate together, I was prepared for high-toned intellectual conversation with this erudite professor, but he did not expound, he queried. He had somehow the air of a bemused uncle who asked and imparted information about life to a promising young person. I liked his kindly, informal way of speaking, his unassuming simplicity. He was entirely unpretentious. He even asked me a surprising question: "Do you believe in fairies?" What manner of man was this, I wondered, meeting his quizzical eyes. "Yes, I always have," I answered and counterqueried, "Do you?" Then we were off into the supernatural and the psychic, in which he said he was interested and about which he would like to know more.

We talked of vegetarianism and I was glad to hear he also was a non-carcass-eater. He said he was a pacifist and did not like killing—of man, bird, or beast. It was this side of him which appealed to me most. I think if he had not been a vegetarian, I would not have tied up with him.

I responded to the intelligent, considerate, humorous, and forthright person he obviously was. He seemed so sane, so surefooted and balanced, so *good*-natured. All this I had the sense to see and absorb on our first trip together.

That evening we took a walk up a country lane. It was a soft September moonlit night. The deep-woods, grassed-over road we had followed wound up a hill lined with flaming maples. We had come to a stopping place, a crossroad, and he asked which I wanted to take: the high road or the low road.

I chose the upper. Then I impulsively turned to him and kissed him. I must have realized it was a real crossroad in my life. Whether our path could be designated high or low, we traveled from there on together.

This was a turning point for me, a surprising move on my part. We had barely met and I gave him this mark of confidence and trust and esteem. He was so earnest, so true, so touching, that I recognized him as kin and acted on impulse. There was never a question then or now in my mind but that this man was and could be a good influence on my life and that I could learn much from him.

What were his feelings at that moment when I kissed him on the cheek? Either I was premeditatedly bold or else singularly innocent and sincere. Mine was the first such move in our future alliance. It was discovery if not love at first sight—a lasting recognition of another person's being as of immense worth and quality. He was to become the most worthwhile person in my life, an ideal lifetime companion.

I found in Scott a person imbued with ideals, dedication, and direction, determined to live at his highest and not to be distracted from his main aim—the general welfare. He was an exemplar, seeking the truth and endeavoring to live it in his daily life. At first sight I had sensed in him these great qualities, plus a genial humanity that showed in his delightful laugh and the twinkle in his eyes, although he could be deadly serious when addressing weighty subjects.

He abhorred gossip and small talk, avoiding commonplace trivia. Like Thoreau, he would not "feebly fabulate and paddle in the social slush." He was not an easy or avid conversationalist, though there was usually a chuckle and a hidden smile lurking back of all he had to say. "I am tired of being educated by Scott," Dorothy Thompson wrote to her husband Sinclair Lewis while she was in Moscow covering the tenth anniversary of the Russian Revolution. "However, one forgives him his earnestness when he smiles, and he sometimes did."

I responded to the resolute goodness I perceived, his knowledge and wisdom, his kindness and consideration. Here was a man I could trust, who knew where he was going and who was on his way, exemplifying, both in his living and in his words, conscious dedicated purpose.

I also felt within myself the need to follow a cause and dedicate myself to an ideal beyond the trivialities of daily suburban existence. Even an unexceptional person, as I knew myself to be, could have stirrings that life might be more than a mere round of daily doings. I had a far-off vision of truth and felt myself to be of the company of seekers. Here was a brother soul, a comrade on the way, from whom I could learn, and whom I could possibly help.

How tell of our lives together? First, something should be said of our backgrounds, the forces—external and internal— which helped to shape our characters. Much of this, in Scott's case, is in his autobiography *The Making of a Radical*, written when he was in his eighties. The tale he tells there delineates many details of his career that will only be touched on here. This will be a recounting of his personal rather than his political and social life, which is found elsewhere in countless articles, in books, and in two biographies.★

This is not a biography of Scott, nor an autobiography, but is offered as a tribute to his being as I knew it. I should like Scott to be known as he was in daily life, as an unassuming, kindly, wise husbandman as well as a principled, uncompromising, intellectual radical. Also I should like to share his peaceful, intentional, and premeditated ending.

Some noteworthy episodes from our lives before we met should be shared, then we come to our life together.

★See the Selected Bibliography at the back of this book.

Scott the Exemplar

> *When one hears of Scott Nearing it is commonly to the effect that some ass of a college president has forbidden him the campus, or some gorilla of a policeman has jailed him for sedition. What our third-rate snivilization fails to estimate at its real worth is the resolute and indomitable devotion of such a man.*
>
> H. L. Mencken, *American Mercury*, 1929

*E*ARLY IN HIS LIFE, even in childhood, Scott had shown concern and solicitude for those who had less in life than he. Born in the upper echelons of society, he felt that the more he had the more he owed to those who had less. He had seen poverty among the workers in local Pennsylvania mines where he had taken jobs and worked with Finnish and Hungarian immigrants who comprised part of the work force in the mine his grandfather ran. Observing and knowing conditions from the inside, when he became a college professor he began to write and speak on the issues of labor and the vast differential in wages and living conditions between workers and employers. As early as 1905, in his twenties, he was speaking publicly on liberal reform. This was his beginning in social service.

"Even before I began the study of Economics," he said in an early lecture, "I was impressed by the monstrous inequality which exists between the rich and the poor in modern society. The rich enjoy wealth, leisure, and boundless opportunity. The poor are overwhelmed by misery, overwork, and insanitation.

The rich have a heaven of opportunity; the poor a hell of misery, and the heaven of the rich is founded upon the hell of the poor.

"If I was impressed by these conditions before I had studied them, I was appalled after having given them careful consideration. I had heard of poverty; I believed that misery and vice existed, but I was not aware that they were prevalent in every town and city of the land. Ability and capacity are suppressed; together with the progress which might well be attained, were opportunity more universal. . . . The poor are ignorant of the fact that by standing together at the ballot box, they might revolutionize conditions in a decade."

Investigation into child labor in Pennsylvania mills and factories shocked him enormously. He felt that a teacher with leisure and learning owed the world a debt; he must speak out. He joined the Pennsylvania Child Labor Committee which sought by legislation and publicity to limit and abolish the practice.

When he took up such questions in public, he stepped on the toes of certain members of the board of trustees of the University of Pennsylvania where he taught, notably those of George Wharton Pepper and J. Levering Jones, two prominent Philadelphians. They decided he was a burr under the skin of authority and on June 16, 1915, summarily dismissed this objectionable upstart of a young professor who was voicing heterodox opinions.

The abrupt dismissal from his nine-year teaching position at the university caused a furor in more than academic circles. The press, the student body, and faculty rose in Scott's defense. One student protested: "He is one of the few men who actually performs the service that the university expects of its teachers: he makes the college men think. A professor who can do this is, in my opinion, worth his weight in gold." A fellow professor wrote: "Here is a man recommended by the dean and faculty for reappointment and who is said to be very much above the average in their judgment in ability, fidelity to work, effectiveness in teaching and in the loyalty he has shown to the institution. For the trustees to dismiss him at the close of the academic year, without notice, may even be of questionable legality. But that it is unusual and unjust is beyond question." Scott's direct superior in the economics department, Simon Patten, testified: "In losing Doctor Nearing the university loses one of its most effective men, a man of extraordinary ability, of superlative popularity and a man who, to my mind, exerted the greatest moral force for good in the university."

The trustees remained adamant. Scott's future in Philadelphia was over. He was cast out for criticizing too freely and too openly the system and the powers that be. As a result of his being ousted from the University of Pennsylvania, no major institution in the country would hire him. The University of Toledo, a small municipal college, fairly liberal in its outlook, offered him an appointment in 1916.

He moved to Ohio with his wife and two small sons and served there as professor of political science and dean of the College of Arts and Sciences for two short years, until war clouds gathered. The First World War was raging in Europe and Scott took a strong antiwar stand. He regarded violence and armed conflict as the most costly way of making social changes, resulting in frightful loss of life and social wealth. He saw war as a power struggle between competitive empires—"organized destruction and mass murder by civilized nations," as he called it. He wrote and spoke accordingly.

When the United States, under Woodrow Wilson—who had vowed to keep the country out of the conflict—joined forces with Britain in the fight, patriotic elements in Toledo made Scott Nearing unwelcome there and in 1917 he was dropped from their institution of higher learning. His reputation was now in shreds, and, although he was not yet forty years old, he was never again to teach in any school in the United States.

A poignant notation from this period of his life was found in Scott's papers. "Must one accept the community's way of life, their moral standards, or can one formulate one's own? Live it, uphold it, swim upstream against the static society? Or follow the path of least resistance? My eleven years of teaching were the best years I ever spent, the happiest and most useful. They were years of intimate personal contact, of strong personal ties. They brought so many satisfactions that as I look back over them I can have no bitter thought—not a single regret. But the door has been shut on that world that I understand better than I understand anything else—and that I loved so well—shut forever, I think."

In an article written for the *New York Call* in 1922, Scott wrote: "The living of an ideal involves the payment of a certain price. . . . The further the ideal is removed from the common practice, the higher the price must be paid for it. . . . If your ideal is to live a mentally active, mentally honest life, to seek the truth, then you may have to sacrifice even food, clothing, and shelter to get it." In another *New York Call* issue, he wrote: "The hermit who goes off to live all alone need not go as a martyr; he makes a choice between one mode of living and another—he is going along another highway and paying toll there."

Here is a handwritten notation from a card in Scott's files: "The majority will always be for caution, hesitation, and the status quo—always against creation and innovation. The innovator—he who leaves the beaten track—must therefore always be a minoritarian—always be an object of opposition, scorn, hatred. It is part of the price he must pay for the ecstasy that accompanies creative thinking and acting."

Vincent van Gogh wrote in a letter to his brother Theo: "One of the reasons that I have been out of employment for years is simply that I have other ideas than the gentlemen who give the places to men who think as they do."

Scott was quite aware of the price he had to pay for following his convictions. He regretted enormously the loss of opportunities as a teacher—to have day-to-day contact with his students and to help develop their thoughts and directions. Lecturing to chance audiences in no way satisfied that lack. Canadian educator David Suzuki wrote in his 1987 book, *Metamorphosis*: "In large lecture halls the intimacy is gone. It is performance rather than sharing of ideas. . . . Exchange of ideas, open discussion and tolerance are the cornerstones of university life. . . . A university course is more than just the transmission and receipt of information. It embodies the teacher's personality: it contains the distillates of his scholarship, research and introspection. Each school-room contact is a sharing of ideas, a very personal gift from the teacher."

Scott had always intended to live a life of dedication and service and commitment, never a life of self-gratification or personal aggrandizement, so he could not be unduly perturbed by his oustings. Pericles, when he was informed of the defeat at Thermopylae, was asked, "How do you take it so cooly, Pericles? Are you really indifferent?" "No, I am not indifferent," he replied. "But of what use is it to strive all one's days for the rhythm of life if it will not support me in adversity? I have endeavored to meet life at all points with serenity and I should be a poor thing if it failed me now." Scott had seen his audiences dwindle till he talked to ten or twelve instead of hundreds or thousands; his readership was cut off and nearly eliminated. He remained equable and worked on persistently. His name and fame became obscure; he kept on producing, undismayed.

Two penciled notes on scraps of paper were found in his files: "(10/20/08) Live in the world; sell thy soul to the Devil and thou shalt succeed; thou shalt be great. Listen to the voice of thy conscience; act according to its summons, fearing nothing, and thou shalt be just. The successful are praised, the great are remembered, the just lay the foundations of eternity." (This may have been for one of his homilies which the widely read *Everybody's* printed regularly on their front page in the early decades of this century.) And here, seemingly, is a note to himself written in 1911: "When you do begin your work you will probably have to show one thing—i.e., that man is of more social importance than are economic goods. The real question then is,—how can this fact be demonstrated?" In the same period Scott wrote another notation to himself: "Simplify and order life; plan ahead; follow the line resolutely; eliminate non-essential things; keep distractions to a minimum; live day by day, bread labor, with nature, with people, establishing worthwhile contacts; collect and organize material; do research and follow trends; write, lecture and teach; keep in close touch with the class struggle; acquire an understanding of basic and cosmic forces; gradually uniting together a unified, integrated, poised personality that is constantly learning and growing."

He was greatly inspired by some thoughts that Olive Schreiner, a feminist, writer, and radical of the late Victorian era, recorded in her memoirs: "I think it is well to resolve in one's early youth that no good shall ever be good to oneself which is bought at the smallest price of one's intellectual integrity. The men who hold by this can never be entirely successful in their generation . . . but one never regrets having stood alone."

In 1917, Scott noted down "a turning point in my life":

1. I become a socialist, a pacifist, a vegetarian.
2. I give up dancing and dress clothes, as symbols of a life I am leaving.
3. I abandon the role of a successful, popular lecturer. William Hard told me: "All you need is a good story to start; two or three good illustrations of your theme; a dramatic gesture to finish. People will always come back for more."

4. I dedicate myself to promote the general welfare, the commonweal, the common good.

Scott had his heroes, according to this list found in his papers.

Tolstoy and self-renunciation
Socrates and the rule of reason
Thoreau and the simplified life
Marx and Engels who were against exploitation
Gandhi and nonviolence
Buddha and harmlessness
Victor Hugo and humanitarianism
Jesus and social service
Confucius and the middle way
Richard Bucke and cosmic consciousness
Walt Whitman and the naturists
Edward Bellamy and the utopians
Olive Schreiner and the allegorists

Scott often liked to quote Robert Louis Stevenson's "It is better to travel hopefully than to arrive, and the greatest success is to labor." The following sentences on file cards may have been his own thoughts as there were no quotation marks:

If your life doesn't end in failure, you haven't reached high enough. [Here Scott added a quotation from H. G. Wells: "So it was failure I had to achieve."]

If a man is one step ahead of the crowd he is a leader; if two steps ahead, he is a disturber; if three steps, he is a fanatic and not to be trusted.

Responsibility for personal contact is taken by those who set up their own value scales, make their own judgments and bide the consequences.

At the time he wrote those lines, Scott was thirty-four. He was in excellent health, ready and eager to practice his teaching profession almost anywhere and with almost any group of students. Yet he was deprived of the opportunity to present his conception of the "live-and-help-live" principle.

He was out of academia, his chosen career in ruins. He had a wife and two children to support. Beginning in 1908 he had written a dozen books, all of which had been issued by prominent publishers and used as textbooks in the public schools. Now these were taken off the market, off school shelves. They brought no further royalty payments. Times were hard for the young ex-professor. His future had seemed secure and promising. A full, auspicious, and interesting life had loomed ahead.

Fate and his own character and actions had taken a hand and cast him forth "onto the rubbish heap of history," as the *Daily Worker* later observed acrimoniously. He was abundantly fitted by training and native abilities and inclination to be a teacher and would remain so all his life, but there was no place for such a cantankerous pedagogue in the established system. He had chosen the hard way, the innovative.

Out and on his own in this epoch of his life, he helped to form and lead an organization called the People's Council for Peace and Democracy, which had a nationwide membership of eight hundred thousand. It was started originally to keep the United States out of the war. After the country entered the war in April 1917, the People's Council changed their emphasis and stressed a war not to the finish but for a negotiated peace.

In 1917 Scott wrote a book called *The Great Madness* analyzing the basic causes and aims of the war as commercial, not idealistic as was vaunted. For this temerity he was indicted by the government, in federal court, ostensibly for obstructing recruitment and enlistment in the armed forces. Newspapers at home and abroad took up the story. Scott pleaded his own case before a federal grand jury, outlining his position sentence by sentence, using his pamphlet as his text. The blue-ribbon jury

acquitted him of treason, but fined the Rand School which had
published and circulated the document. (The full trial, including Scott's address to the jury, was printed by Rand School
Press in 1917. Scott's address to the jury has been reprinted in
A Scott Nearing Reader.★)

On the day of acquittal, Scott left the courtroom and went
out into the hall to telephone his mother that he would not be
imprisoned. (At the time, the court had been passing out
twenty-four-year terms for opposition to the war.) A court attendant stopped him, saying with a strong Irish brogue, "It may
not be becoming of me to say this to you, sir, but if it weren't
for you and the likes of you, the likes of me would be in chains
and we know it."

Though acquitted, Scott's name as a troublemaker was now
known nationwide and his reputation was so notorious that he
could hope for no more teaching positions anywhere. His ideas,
so freely expressed, were dangerous to existing institutions. If
he could not teach in academia he would instruct where he
could, on itinerant circuits. He accepted, from whatever source,
requests to speak. If no fee was attached, he would still go,
often paying his own expenses. He did not talk for money; he
talked to teach.

His lectures were always factual and practical. In *The Making
of a Radical*, he wrote:

> Beginning with the war of 1917–18 I deliberately stopped intro-
> ducing any form of lightness or humor into my talks. I stopped
> being a "successful and pleasing lecturer." I went onto the plat-
> form, presented my material in as clear a way as possible, said
> what I had to say and let it go at that. I no longer tried to ingra-
> tiate myself with audiences or with the organizations sponsoring
> the lectures. Before each lecture I said to myself: "This is the last

★Edited by Steve Sherman. Foreword by Helen K. Nearing. Metuchen,
N.J.: Scarecrow Press, 1989.

time I shall appear on this platform"; then I went ahead and said what I had to say, letting the chips fall where they would. And very often my first talk was my last one on that platform. For instance, at Cooper Union in New York City I gave a provocative talk on war and revolution. They never asked me again.

Through the years Scott continued writing, but was no longer published by prestigious or commercial publishers. He had to find small publishing houses or have his books printed at his own expense and distributed privately. He no longer could contribute to magazines or get his books reviewed, or even stocked in bookshops. His name was so reprehensible that three widely divergent newspapers, the *New York Times*, the *Christian Science Monitor*, and the *Daily Worker* refused paid advertisements for his books.

He was really on his own, at the bottom of the pit. No school, no party, no organization or institution would have him —and none satisfied his visionary standards. He was recently separated from wife and family: when they broke up he turned over all of the family property to them and started life anew with a small amount of cash and the equity in his life insurance policies. He was then completely alone.

It was at that low period of his life that I met Scott.

Helen the Free Spirit

Would more natures were like thine,
so divinely wild and free.

from my 1921 high school class book

I CHOSE a very good family to be born into in 1904. My parents were intellectuals, leaders, or members of every liberal and educational organization in the small residential town of Ridgewood, New Jersey. I, my older brother Alec, and my younger sister Alice were brought up in a congenial home with every comfort and opportunity available. Harmony must have been evident, as C. Jinarajadasa, a prominent Ceylonese visitor, wrote in our 1909 guestbook: "I envy the parents their children, the children their parents, and all their bungalow."

My Dutch mother, Maria Obreen, was a painter, brought up in Holland, where her uncle was Director of the famous Rijksmuseum in Amsterdam. She lived in the mansion back of the museum, giving her access whenever she wished to the masterpieces and studios. My father, Frank Knothe, was a successful New York businessman with primarily scholarly interests. He had a literary turn of mind and was also very musical, with a fine tenor voice.

In 1896, in her early twenties, Maria had sailed away from Amsterdam to America to escape from three suitors in order to decide which, if any, to marry. She met Frank Knothe at a gathering in New York City soon after her arrival in the New

World. He fell in love with the lovely young Dutch woman. A pastel portrait from this time, showing her modest downcast face with delicate blonde tendrils, now hangs in our home in Maine.

The couple bicycled together in the Berkshires to get acquainted. Maria returned to Holland, not to her former suitors, but on her honeymoon with her handsome American husband.

The young couple had many ideals in common—mental and spiritual outlooks—beyond the usual levels of their contemporaries in the 1880s and 1890s. They were "flower children" of their time. For ethical as well as health reasons both were vegetarians, preferring not to eat the bodies of their animal brothers. They meditated, which few Americans then did. They believed in reincarnation as a reasonable possibility and experimented in spiritualism. They were nonconformists, open to unorthodox ideas. They were members of the Theosophical Society, which is where and how they had met, at a local meeting.

Theosophy is not a religion; it is described as a universal brotherhood without distinction of race, color, sex, caste, or creed. It purports to be the ancient wisdom, the philosophy that underlies all religions. It integrates the esoteric aspects of Buddhism, Hinduism, Mohammedanism, Judaism, Zoroastrianism, and Christianity—all religions being paths to the truth and no one religion containing the whole. It offers a philosophy which renders life intelligible and puts forward a code of ethics that is not merely a collection of moral verities but a practical way to live together in peace. The Theosophical Society is a worldwide nonsectarian organization of seekers after truth, which is what Maria and Frank Knothe considered themselves to be.

They settled down in New York City, but on the birth of their third child wisely moved out to the suburbs of New Jersey to raise the young ones in pleasanter, healthier surroundings.

There the family stayed through the children's growth to young adulthood.

Their country place had lawns and a pine grove, and they established extensive gardens. An East Indian bungalow was built to their own design on their ample acreage. The house had broad verandahs and was spacious inside with timbered ceilings, fireplaces, nooks for reading, and oriental rugs and Japanese prints for decoration.

The young couple were out of the ordinary in that small suburban village. To their deep interest in music, art, and literature was added an inclination to social service. They joined local organizations, contributing time and money to philanthropic causes. They were acknowledged as useful citizens and interested participants in town business. My father was president of the local board of education, the Unitarian Men's Club, and the men's chorus of the Orpheus Club; my mother, president of the Ridgewood Women's Club. He, head of the local Red Cross; she, head of the Society for the Prevention of Cruelty to Animals; and so forth. From youth on I was made aware of the possibilities of a life of social significance, of involvement in social causes.

The Knothes were also unique in the village because they maintained at that time a large garden from which the family was provided with fresh, organic, wholesome food. In the early years of this century most Americans did not question the meaty, starchy, saladless national diet. They filled their stomachs with what they were used to, what they liked, and left reasoning and questioning and ethics to philosophers. The rights of the animals they consumed were rarely if ever thought of. Enzymes, vitamins, and calories were not considered seriously. Food was food, down with it. No questions asked.

Frank and Maria, and perforce their children, ate no meat, no fish or poultry, though eggs and milk were included in their diet. All their foods were homegrown when possible. The garden was maintained by Philip, the gardener, with fresh fruits and vegetables daily on the table. Their cook baked whole wheat bread and used only brown sugar and brown rice, also unusual for that time. I was the only one of the children who kept up these practices. The others lapsed at various times and later conformed completely to the "rules" of an ordinary diet.

My brother and sister were conformists to neighborhood habits in nearly every way. They never fitted easily into the vegetarian, literary, musical, or occult trends and the intellectual propensities of our parents as I did. Alec, the firstborn, was exceedingly competent manually, building model airplanes as a small boy. He went on to develop exceptional mechanical abilities, becoming a skilled pilot in South America, later owning his own flying school in Florida. Alice, my younger sister, was an easygoing, sociable child, content to live on the periphery of our parents' deeper interests. She developed considerable talent in interior decoration, was good-looking, and dressed well in stylish clothes of her own making. She married early and is still living happily with her congenial husband. They built various homes in New Jersey, Vermont, and Florida, which she decorated. They have children and grandchildren and live a normal, prosperous, comfortable American life.

We three got along well enough but had little in common except family affairs. They considered me an oddity, always reading, and I was far from mechanical or stylish. Later in my life politics and unconventional behavior kept them wary of my ways. One thing we concurred in: a great love and appreciation for our mother. She was the harmonious heart of the family. Our father, rather removed from us by his business preoccupations in the city, was our mentor and model, and the kindly provider of all good things.

I remember little of my early childhood except constant

care by nurses and my mother, poring over books before I could properly read, playing at paper dolls with Alice, and adoring teddy bears, which I much preferred to dolls. Why can I not remember more? Seasons and years went by for the small girl and there is nothing in my memory to show for them all but short episodes: twilight evenings piping songs with my father out in our summer house; toiling up three flights of gas-lit stairs to grandma's New York City apartment; displaying proudly a horridly pink sweater to neighbors across the street, and pussycats aplenty.

Who and what was I all that time? What was I up to? Apparently I was a quiet unobtrusive child satisfied with my own company but also taking part in the group that congregated at our bungalow—a gathering place for all the neighborhood children—where we played games of hide-and-seek, tag, and croquet and roller-skated or ice-skated on our flooded tennis court in winter.

On my fifth birthday, February 23, 1909, my father inscribed to his "Beloved Daughter" a collection of "Poems to Think About" in a 1907 edition of *The Children's Hour*. So began my exposure to and interest in literature. A subscription to a child's popular magazine of the time, *St. Nicholas*, and twelve volumes of *The Book of Knowledge*, for me and my brother and sister, became dog-eared from constant reading. I was addicted to books and reading from then on.

A Dutch cousin and a good violinist came over from Holland, staying with us for a year when I was still a child. She brought a small violin as a gift, on which I was soon playing well. This was a great joy to my father who foresaw for me a possible musical career that he was not able to pursue for himself. I had the best teachers in the vicinity and showed real promise, performing locally while in my teens.

When I was thirteen, my parents sent me to a girls' camp in New Hampshire to partly wean me from my bookishness.

There I changed so that my mother, meeting me at the station, remarked, "She has blossomed into another child." Being away from the family, I had developed a personality of my own. I canoed alone a great deal on the lake while the other girls frolicked and socialized on the dock. I found I preferred the company of silent trees and rocks to the groups of raucous gigglers. I was a loner, though never lonely. At camp I learned to draw, wrote poetry, played my violin extensively, and even composed tunes for singing.

Two knowledgeable counselors at the camp introduced me to the works of the Irish storyteller Lord Dunsany, to Algernon Blackwood's fanciful tales and Walter De la Mare's poems. They added a taste for the fey and fantastic to my already awakened interest in Browning's poetry. I developed many interests at that age such as reading people's palms and defining their characters from the length of their fingers and the depth and position of their lines. I studied handwriting and collected autographs for their scripts, not necessarily for their notoriety. I utilized dictionaries early on and constantly looked up the origins and derivations of words. I was surprisingly inquiring and did not accept unquestioningly the world in which I found myself.

I would observe a chair as a strange four-legged object. Human forms with two flapping tentacles and nose-centered faces I saw as weird—not accepting them as normal obvious shapes. I lived in a world of science fiction before I knew science fiction existed. The whole world was miraculous and astonishing to me and I took none of it for granted. Continual wonder was one of my developing qualities. I was, at that age, in tune with words I later found to have been voiced by Einstein: "One of the most beautiful things we can experience is the mysterious. . . . It is the source of all true science and art. He who can no longer pause to wonder is as good as dead."

To the surprise of my family, after the camp experience I changelinged from an introspective introvert and a scrawny preadolescent to a lively, effervescent character, becoming known for my odd nature and original behavior. My old-time childhood nickname of "Sis"—to distinguish me from the two other Helens on the block—was changed in school to "Knutty," partly derived from the family name, Knothe (pronounced "Ken-*oh*-thee"), and partly because of my unusual ways. I was considered odd by my classmates. I was a vegetarian not only because my parents were but because I loved animals and refused to eat them. I had many pets, notably cats, which I adored for their furry coats, their purring, their tails, their pointed ears, their long whiskers, and their paws like raspberries. I was a member of the student council, yet played truant many days for long solitary walks, reporting my truant time to the principal. Though a reclusive reader and musician, I was athletic, played basketball, and was a good runner and ice skater.

English was my favorite subject. I remember memorizing and reciting in school some of Browning's poems, particularly three. From his "The Lost Leader": "Just for a handful of silver he left us, just for a riband to stick in his coat . . ."

From *Pippa Passes*: "Day! / Faster and more fast, / O'er night's brim, day boils at last: / Boils, pure gold, o'er the cloud-cap's brim / Where spurting and suppressed it lay, / For not a froth-flake touched the rim / Of yonder gap in the solid gray / Of the eastern cloud, an hour away; / But forth one wavelet, then another, curled, / Till the whole sunrise, not to be suppressed, / Rose, reddened, and its seething breast / Flickered in bounds, grew gold, then overflowed the world. // Oh, Day, if I squander a wavelet of thee, . . ."

And notably, from "*Prospice*": "Fear death?—to feel the fog in my throat, / The mist in my face, / When the snows begin, and the blasts denote / I am nearing the place, / The power of the night, the press of the storm, / The post of the foe; . . ."

Quite some choices, I now think, for a young girl.

My first sixteen years were carefree and insouciant. I romped through school, finding it easy, and did not overburden myself with studying. For wide reading outside school I used my parent's large library, which ranged from Bacon's essays through Shakespeare to the philosophies of Emerson and William James to the novels of Robert Louis Stevenson and to contemporary writers.

Into numerous scrapbooks I collected countless poems and pictures and stories from my parents' constant influx of literary magazines, journals, and papers. Some of these bulging books of childhood and adolescent compendia are still in my present library.

As little more than a child I pounced on felicitous phrases and apt quotations as I read, underlining and later copying them onto cards for my files. This habit has continued all through my life and proved invaluable for my later researches and writings. My diaries and numerous scrapbooks contain rather profound items for a callow teenager. Apparently early on I felt there was power and purpose in the universe and queried what we are here for and what it was all about.

I always had a deep desire to contribute and to live rightly. Here are a few gleanings, careless as to author, from my early collections that reveal my thinking at the time. The only quote with a clue to its source is the last one, from Walt Whitman's 1855 preface to *Leaves of Grass*.

Life is a school, exactly adapted to your lesson.

Your present life is only a chapter out of the middle of a book. You have written previous chapters and you will write later ones. You are your own author.

The love of one's country is a natural thing. But why stop at the border?

So think as if your every thought were to be etched in fire upon the sky for all and everyone to see. And so in truth it is.

So speak as if the world entire were but a single ear intent on hearing what you say. And so in truth it is.

So do as if your every deed were to recoil upon your head. And so in truth it does.

So live as if your God himself had need of you, his life to live. And so in truth He does.

Love the earth and sun and the animals, despise riches, give alms to every one that asks, stand up for the stupid and crazy, devote your income and labor to others, hate tyrants, argue not concerning God, have patience and indulgence toward the people, take your hat off to nothing known or unknown or to any man or number of men, go freely with powerful uneducated persons and with the young and with the mothers of families, read these leaves in the open air every season of every year of your life, re-examine all you have been told at school or church or in any book, dismiss whatever insults your own soul. . . .

Eventually I began venturing to write a bit myself, as I became first the Joke Editor and then Literary Editor of my high school paper the *Arrow*. Here is the first verse of my "Ode to Latin," a subject in which I did not excel in my freshman year.

> Oh Latin, base language, and would you elide me,
> To slip and to slide and to swiftly glide by me?
> But I'll get you yet, you infidel tongue,
> With your stella, stellarum and aedificum.

Another poem I wrote for the high school paper was a parody of Robert Burns' "To a Mouse, On turning up her nest with the plough, November 1785." Mine was titled "To a Worm, Upon cutting one in half, September 1920."

Wee, icky, slimy, slithery one,
Thy little life on earth is done,
No more shalt thou set eyes on sun,
    Nor course pursue
All through my mother's apples run,
    To thine own rue.

Alas, an' 'twas no fault of mine!
On applesauce we were to dine:
Your little home was my design—
    Not your young life.
And you must to your fate resign
    Or blame the knife.

I doubt no' but that you have found
A wormies' happy hunting ground,
Where you can dig in mound on mound,
    Serene to dwell,
Where no disturbing thought or sound
    Breaks in your cell.

But wormie, if thou found it hard:
Think of my nervous system jarred
On contact with you, little pard.
    Your oozy feel!
Next time I will be on my guard—
    No apples peel.

Meanwhile my violining continued. I gave music my principal attention, practicing regularly, with weekly lessons. I played at school and church affairs and obbligatoed my father's fine voice. We enjoyed musicking together. He had never had the chance to learn the piano in his youth, but his love for music and my playing was so great that he learned to accompany me with tapes on his electric Pianola, and often soothed me to sleep when I was in my adjoining room with Chopin nocturnes, Beethoven adagios, and Rubinstein melodies. I remember listening to his playing long into the night. Through him I was born and bred to books and music and kept a love of them all my life.

While I was still sixteen, my parents asked me if, when I graduated from high school, I would want to attend the Boston Conservatory of Music, or go to Vassar College, or study the violin in Europe. I at once chose the latter, although not many girls of my age lived and traveled abroad alone at that time.

At seventeen, leaving those days behind, I sailed on the S.S. *Ryndam* with my mother on July 2, 1921, just two weeks out of school. We landed in Rotterdam and a new expanding life opened before me.

Soon after our arrival in Europe, my mother took me to an international Theosophical convention in Paris. Mrs. Annie Besant, a prominent Englishwoman, was president of the society and presided. She knew my parents from lecture trips in the United States and had seen me in the cradle in Ridgewood, so we met again.

One of the speakers at the conference was Jiddu Krishnamurti, a young Hindu who had been taken up by Mrs. Besant and introduced to the world as a vehicle for the coming World Teacher. He was not proclaimed as the Teacher himself, but as the body to be used and spoken through, as Jesus' body was supposed by Theosophists to have been used by the Christ.

I heard the then shy young man speak. He was slight, of average height and, being Indian, his coloring was dark. His hair was black and glossy, his features were classic, with aquiline nose, great fringed eyes, and a sensitive mouth. I remembered little of what he said, only the slight, dark, handsome figure on the vast illuminated stage and his halting delivery at that time. From my box overlooking the platform there was of course no thought of my seeing or hearing him again.

Before my mother returned to the United States, Mrs. Besant made it possible for me to be admitted to the highly prestigious Theosophical Headquarters building at Amsteldyk 76, in Amsterdam, where I was to live and study for the next couple of years. Once acclimated to the new surroundings and language, I took hold, practiced regularly at my violin, and benefited from the teaching of Louis Zimmerman, concertmaster of Willem Mengelberg's Concertgebouw Orchestra and the best violin teacher in Holland. My talent was evident; would I develop into a competent professional player? That was now up to me.

The Young Impressionable Krishnamurti

It is the going out from oneself that is love and not the accident of its return. It is the expedition, whether it fail or succeed.

H. G. Wells, *First and Last Things*, 1908

THE PART of my life concerned with Krishnamurti is so removed from the later part with Scott that I am loath to bring it up at all. It is an inconclusive story of happenings that lifted me sometimes to supernal heights and then dropped me down to earth with a bang. But if only an episode, lasting a few years, this experience still influenced what I later became in the person who met Scott, and should be included in this story of living, learning, loving, and leaving.

I am a fairly private person, keeping myself to myself. I rarely talk about personal things. My memories and thoughts are private possessions which I do not yield easily to others. When asked, I do not like to expound on my previous intimacy with Krishnamurti, and never thought I would write of this or make it known. When queried as to the years of our close contact I usually answer: "He was a unique person and I was privileged to know him," and let it go at that.

Why and how tell of a love long gone and long superseded for me by a much stronger love, more lasting and completely companionable? The earlier love was passionate and compelling and professed to be eternal. It lasted, full of protestations of undying devotion, for half a dozen years, then sank into cool acquaintance, finally to nonrecognition. What we had was lovely while it lasted, with an exquisite beginning, but with a needlessly callous ending.

Is it seemly and proper to recount and expose happenings that are long gone by—that were seemingly erased from his mind and memory in later years—now that Krishnamurti is dead and cannot refute or deny the facts? But facts there are in dozens of letters and notes written to me and still in my possession. I tell of it now because my life was undoubtedly influenced by him, and there are stories in print, in others' reminiscences, and in novels, which describe our relationship inadequately or in false colors.

When he first met me, he was guileless, innocent and pure, exquisitely ardent, overwhelmed with the new emotions stirring in him. His followers of later years, when he decried and belittled personal attachments, would be astonished to know of the concentrated force of his emotions for this slip of a girl. Those to whom he is now a guiding light might even welcome a heretofore unknown insight into his early predilections and affections.

This youthful love was an intriguing if ephemeral part of his life and might well be added to the known accounts of his life and career. His letters to me, written in the 1920s, reveal some of his low periods, some of his fantasies and dreams of the time. His lengthy missives, some of them ten and twelve pages long, were naive and repetitive, more full of yearnings and endearments than news of his activities. They may be noteworthy only in that they were written by a youth who later became a man of stature and importance to thousands of people all over the globe.

Would Krishnamurti have wanted these things made public? At one time he asked me to burn his letters. When I wailed, he said "Keep them. They are yours. My love goes with them." In an interview given to Rom Landau much later on in 1937 and published in Landau's *God Is My Adventure*, he succinctly gave permission for any part of himself to be revealed: "There is no privacy in my life, and everyone may hear any detail that may interest them. You can ask anything you want, the most tactless, the most intimate questions." He went on to say, "You asked me just now about personal love and my answer is that I no longer know it. Personal love does not exist for me."

In a certain sense the whole experience *was* an impersonal one. Who it was who received his love and letters was unimportant and irrelevant. Another girl or young woman appearing in the same place at the same time might have served as well and acted as a catalyst. Krishnamurti was ready when he encountered the needed touchstone.

In *A Midsummer Night's Dream*, the fairy queen Titania becomes enamored of a yokel with an ass's head. Under enchantment, whomever she first sighted was to be her love. What magic was afoot when Krishnamurti met this girl in Holland? He was poised and ready for an appearance. He was looking for love and understanding and he found it.

[Here I think I'll shift to third gear and third person.]

Before starting her violin studies in Holland in earnest, Helen went that first European summer of 1921 to a Practical Idealist's camp in Ommen, northern Holland. There young people from all over Europe gathered on the banks of the river Vecht to voice and practice their ideas, hopes, and plans for a better world. They were early hippies and she fitted happily into their group, her life opening up to new and important influences.

Krishnamurti was visiting Ommen, staying at Castle Eerde, invited by Baron Philip Van Pallandt, the owner of most of the surrounding township. Van Pallandt was a fervent and dedicated member of the Theosophical Society and wanted to put his extensive estate to some idealistic use. He had thought of turning it over to the International Boy Scout movement, but when he heard of Krishnamurti and his expected mission as World Teacher, Van Pallandt decided to offer him his land for an international campsite.

Krishnamurti was driven around by Baron Van Pallandt to see the sights of Holland. One of the sights he saw was Helen, near the Ommen camp, running and winning a race with a Swedish competitor. Helen had an autograph book with her and asked the two visiting celebrities to sign it. She was then and there invited by the Baron to come and dine at the castle, where she helped fasten a diamond dog collar on the Baron's aristocratic mother. The two young people were attracted to each other from the start. For the week he still had in Holland, Helen and Krishna were constant companions.*

He was extremely taken with the lively girl and before the week was over had avowed his love for her in shy and hesitant terms. He was at that time a very modest, bashful, and boyish youth, although nine years her senior. He had already a small book to his credit, *At the Feet of the Master*, and while not yet a world figure, was beginning to be recognized.

Helen and Krishna walked, talked, and bicycled together over the moors and heather fields. They drove through the dense pine forests of Eerde in Baron Van Pallandt's Rolls Royce. They laughed and joked together and thoroughly enjoyed each other's company.

On the last day of their week together they were on a hillock in the dunes. Krishna covered his face with a handker-

*Later in his life he was "Krishnaji," with the honorific "ji" added by those who revered him. In her time Helen knew him only as "Krishna."

chief to give him the courage to express himself. He told her that in that short time she had joined the trinity of his loves: Annie Besant, whom he called Amma; his beloved brother, Nitya, who was ill in Switzerland with incipient tuberculosis, but who otherwise would have come with him to Holland; and Lady Emily Lutyens, a longtime English friend who had sponsored and been close to the brothers ever since they had left India.

Helen liked Krishna very much. How could she not? His looks were peerless, his thoughts and emotions noble, his manner earnest, if boyish. But she was slower to grow into the strong feelings that so overwhelmed him in that short time. What she felt was far warmer than friendship, yet less than his compelling love.

Here was an insignificant schoolgirl of no great distinction or looks, yet loved at first sight. The feelings he tried to express that August afternoon in Holland were something much greater than a romantic summertime love. She was amazed that he should single her out, and found his love rare and incredible. He, on his part, was overcome with the novelty and strength of his flood of emotions. At twenty-six he had never been in love until this astounding passion had come to him for the young American girl of seventeen.

Krishna's time was up in Holland. He had to return to his ill brother in Montesano, then go to England, and later that year to India. What would happen to their love? When would they meet again? "How very curious," he wrote her on the train leaving her for the first time, "a week ago I did not know you and now it seems I have known you for ages. . . . I am thinking of you *all* the time. Ommen was entirely composed of you, for me, and I wish we were there again."

From Montesano he wrote, "I found two letters awaiting me, both from the person I most wished to have—you. I nearly yelled with pleasure. Don't be afraid. I didn't, as there was my brother and Mr. Cordes with me also. So I controlled myself and did not behave like a child."

From Switzerland he went to London and there arranged one more trip to Holland before the long sea voyage to India. Many letters crossed the English Channel between them during the interim. He came back to Amsterdam especially to see her and was laden with gifts of Indian cloths, gramophone records (of Myra Hess on the clavichord, parts of *The Beggar's Opera*, and some Gilbert and Sullivan operettas—all of which were great favorites of his). He also brought an old copy of *Alice in Wonderland*, with "curiouser and curiouser" written on the fly-leaf, and *The Oxford Book of English Verse*, with an inscription denoting that he could never forget her:

> Tell the grassy hollow that holds the
> bubbling spring-well.
> Tell it to forget the source that
> keeps it fill'd.
> Helen
> Krishna
> Nov: 6: 21

He gave a talk in Amsterdam while he was there, and handed over to Helen his notes in a laborious longhand. He disliked public speaking intensely at that time and mostly read his talks. Later in life, after having given thousands upon thousands of lectures, he was to propound easily on the platform for hours at a time without a single note, and even without any preparation.

Before he left Amsterdam on this last visit, Krishna wrote out directives for Helen's future conduct in life. Here are his admonitions:

> You must be great, not because it may bring you power & pleasure, but because, intrinsically, it is right.

You must be great & magnificent in all things, both small & big, because my love for you is immense, pure & noble. Love, if it is great, should always bring out the great & purifying principles in you.

I should like my dearest friends, whom I love greatly, to be perfect in *all* things they undertake to do.

You must keep your body as clean & as pure as your conscience.

The evolution of the body is as important as the development of your higher self.

Beauty of the body is of the utmost importance for it showeth that thy greater self is also striving after greater beauty.

Look after your body thoroughly well: clean food, sufficient but not too much; & clean hands, feet, teeth, hair; plenty of sleep. Take exercise every morning for about 20 minutes.

Never be influenced by *anybody*, not even by your dearest friend.

All your friends must be pure in mind & body.

Influence by others, however good, is bad, for you must develop your own will power & find your own ideals.

Don't be ever depressed but if you are, retire to your room & get it over.

Do not ever show your depression.

Always have a cheerful face, even when it hurts.

Do not let *anybody* come between you & your ideals.

You *must* play wonderfully well the violin.

You are great & you must be great, so you must be great at playing the violin.

Practice, *regularly*, every day.

You have, beyond any doubt, the will power to do anything you like. Do not waste it.

Be well dressed *always*.

And he left a final, loving note before departing for India:

Amsterdam: Nov: 14: 21.

Darling Helen,

I love you with all my heart & soul & shall *always* do so.

Bless you.

Krishna

They promised to write to each other and there followed a spate of letters that would continue going back and forth for half a dozen years. His letters were the pure and passionate outpourings of a young man who felt extreme affection for a girl. "My devotion for you will last forever & that is why I care so infinitely what you are, what you think & what you do. I love you eternally." And, "Be as fresh as a flower that no one has smelt and as observant as a hawk that is famished. Happy & determined. And then you will make me immeasurably happy. Of that you have no idea."

The initial letter he wrote from India was dated December 4, 1921.

"My own dearest Helen," it began. "Naturally the very first letter from me from Adyar must be to you." He described his tumultuous and garlanded arrival in Bombay with Mrs. Besant as "shaking hands, prostrations, smiles, photos, receptions, all in my honor. I got into Indian clothes as soon as I could. A wonderful turban was tied onto me as I had forgotten how to do it." In Madras "crowds of people threw flowers into the car. I sat there blushing and feeling stupid and emotional. They expect such a lot of things & I feel that I am incapable to gratify their desires."

Helen received a letter from Mrs. Besant, written from Adyar.

About Krishna, dear, I know something of the tie between you. He will help you immensely, I know, but the affection may have a good deal of pain in it, from the ordinary standpoint. He has a great work to do and it may keep him much from you physically. For the world needs him and he cannot, as it were, belong to any one of us. Are you big enough and strong enough, I wonder, to help him and not to hinder him? Try to make your love for him a love that will help him on his path, often a very hard one, and try to live near his level, a very high one. May Master bless and help you, child, and make you strong.

With love, dear Helen,

Annie Besant

What was Helen doing and thinking and reading all this time? The violin, of course, came first, and every day in the headquarters library she practiced for hours. The books on the bookshelves which lined the walls fascinated her. She read the titles as she paced up and down the long room playing her scales and arpeggios. She noted mentally what she would like to read that night unless she went to an evening concert. She attended the Concertgebouw orchestral performances every Thursday evening and Sunday afternoon, happily educating and glutting herself on the great symphonies of Mozart, Mahler, Bach, Beethoven, and Brahms. Her reading consisted largely of Theosophical books on cosmogony, yoga, and philosophy. She had no friends her own age but cheerfully adapted herself to the old folks who lived in the same building, who spoke English so well that it was months before she learned much Dutch.

She loved living in Europe and had few thoughts of home and Ridgewood, except when she wrote to family and friends there. Her life was as she wished it: Krishna for a far-off love, her music as a developing force, and the scope of her interests widening. She was anxious to grasp her opportunities and was appreciative of what had been done for her. The happiest part of her days was running down the steep stairs from her room on the third floor and finding word from Krishna in the mailbox.

What did those passionate outpourings mean to the young girl who received them? Obviously she treasured them, as she kept many of his letters through almost seventy years of moving around the world. Even the first fragile envelope sent in 1921 to Amsterdam is still preserved.

None of Helen's letters remain to show what she may have contributed to the correspondence, but it could not have been much. Those letters must have been affectionate, artless, and no doubt immature. She loved, but did she know what love was? She cared, but felt a surprising detachment for so young and ingenuous a girl. She seemed to know and acknowledge the affair was exceptional, but was curiously uninvolved as to the outcome. Did this show a lack in her? Perhaps to some extent, but it might also show that she sensed the future, his future, and never gave her heart completely to someone she could not partner.

His devotion at the time was evident. But what could become of their affection? There was little background and no future to grow in. He was the World Teacher-Elect and was to travel continually with new scenes and new people and new objectives always before him. What could her role be but a handmaiden, an attendant to be kept in the background? Marriage was never thought of or discussed. She felt she was to be there for him and that was enough. They lived in the present and she was content with that. A human, clinging, possessive love on her part it was not, but rather a supportive, helpful role when needed. He called out; she responded. She was everything he wanted at that time, and everything he gave her filled her. The initiative and plenitude were all his.

Her work on the violin continued in Holland. She constantly attended concerts and moved in musical as well as Theosophical circles. During the winter of 1922 she heard an accomplished Irish violinist, Mary Dickinson-Auner, play at a private recital. Inspired by the artist's playing and interpretations, Helen asked if she could study with her if she ever got to Vienna where Mrs. Auner lived. As it turned out, an international Theosophical congress was to be held that coming summer in Vienna and various notables from the Amsteldyk Headquarters were going early to prepare for it. Helen went with them in February, was installed in the Auner household in Neuwaldegg, a suburb of Vienna on the edge of the Wienerwald, and immediately accelerated studies under this new master. A greater phase of her musical experience opened with chamber music taking a big part.

Her favorite composers then and later included: Beethoven, Bach, Mozart's crystal clarities, all of Brahms, Mahler's sensuous tones, Vaughan Williams's ethereal melodies, Bartok's and Shostakovich's angles and quirks, and Britten's remarkable sonorities. As a schoolgirl she had started out with a passion for opera and Caruso, whose "Pagliacci" score she purchased with high school prize money. In Holland, deeming operatics to be adolescent fare, she graduated to deeper musicality through her constant attendance at the Concertgebouw performances under Mengelberg's direction. Her musical education was becoming full and well-rounded. She began to progress rapidly in her studies and a professional career seemed likely.

Theosophy and Krishnamurti intervened.

The convention was held in July of 1923 in Vienna. Krishna and his brother Nitya, Lady Emily Lutyens, and an entourage of her daughters and other young people came. They urged Helen to stop her eternal practicing and spend more time with them. After some soloing and playing the Bach Double Concerto with Mary Dickinson-Auner at the congress, Helen did leave Neuwaldegg and went with the group to Ehrwald, a village high in the Austrian Tirol where a chalet had been rented in gorgeous mountain surroundings. There she spent the rest of the summer.

In Ehrwald a great decision had to be made: whether to carry on with her music or to follow Krishna and his mission in life. It was a question which went to the core of Helen's beliefs and being. Was music enough? Did she aim to spend her life developing her talent in that direction? Even if she reached full professional status, was this to be her whole objective and her complete fulfillment? Was not the violin, as Krishna had said to her, for only one lifetime, whereas the spiritual path and Theosophy was her true, deep, and abiding interest?

Krishna was insistent that there were many good violinists in the world but that he hoped she would go beyond that and work with him. He wanted her to leave Europe and American influences, go to India with him and then on to Sydney, Australia. There in the Manor above Mosman Bay lived C. W. Leadbeater, who had been a very great influence on Krishna's early years and who had been the first to spot his uniqueness. C. W. L., as he was called, was head of a community in Sydney of mostly young people who were being prepared for "The Work" and were striving to lead exalted lives. Theirs was what would now be called a spiritual commune.

Helen wrote to Mrs. Besant, seeking advice, and received several letters in reply.

> I see no reason why you should devote yourself only to music. If you should have the opportunity of going to Australia —to Sydney—you should seize it. . . . In many ways I should think it would be useful for your future to be for a time in the great centre at Sydney. It would help, as nothing else can, the growth of the inner life, and bring you into touch with your fu- ture co-workers, young men and women about your age. . . . But

I do not see how anyone can decide for you what you should do. It must depend on your inner feelings. Do you care enough for the spiritual life and for the helping of humanity to give up everything else for that aim? That is the real question. To answer it in the affirmative there must be the all-compelling urge that will not be denied.

There was little doubt now in Helen's mind as to what she wanted to do. She would like to devote herself to learning the meaning and purpose of life, then to contribute what she could to its unfolding. She subscribed wholeheartedly to the noble truths Theosophy enumerated: ". . . that the soul of man is immortal and its future is the future of a thing whose growth and splendor has no limit; that the principle which gives life dwells in us and without us, is undying and eternally beneficent. It is not heard or seen but is perceived by those who desire perception; that each man is his own absolute lawgiver, the dispenser of glory or gloom to himself, the decreer of his life, his reward, his punishment." (Mabel Collins, *The Idyll of the White Lotus*.)

Believing in these doctrines, she could live anywhere, work at any occupation, and still fulfill her purpose—and yet, if she devoted herself more completely to the inner life rather than the outer, she would reach her goal sooner and be able to play her part more consciously and effectively. She believed that she had been "called" not to the violin, but to a higher charge. In a sense, the choice had been made at her birth, perhaps even before. She had entered a Theosophical family where she had encountered occult interests early on. Good karma had given her this home and special opportunities. She had met and been recognized as one of the members of an inner group. Why deny and abandon all of that? She vibrated to esoteric knowledge even more deeply than to the most beautiful music, as much as music meant to her. What stirred her most was news of the beyond, of a life transmuted from the physical to the ineffable.

Helen was persuaded while in Ehrwald that Krishna really needed her and she him. She spent all the evening hours during the summer of 1923 with him, witnessing and assisting at strange happenings. Krishna was undergoing intense spiritual ordeals involving his physical body as well as his psyche, and she and Nitya were the only ones of the household who were closeted with him at those times. After supper in Villa Sonnblick the whole group would sit quietly on the balcony, gazing at the mountains and sometimes chanting Indian songs and mantras. Then Nitya would call Helen into the house to find Krishna sometimes unconscious, sometimes moaning and groaning, with apparently intense pains in his spine and head.

The body she found in the room accepted her as its mother and between bouts of agony, held her hand or body close. Most of the time it seemed as though a body-elemental, a creature self, was undergoing the suffering, and not the Krishnamurti of his daily life. The voice was different, the expressions different. It seemed another being—a child self—and she came to love it dearly.

Krishna seemed to be out of his body, which alone endured the pains. At the end of these sessions he remembered little of his cries, moans, even shrieks, and inquired as to what had gone on. He opined it must be the kundalini energy coiled up like a serpent at the base of his spine, which burns its way to the top of the head. It seemed a transcendent purificatory experience, though his physical being was wracked in the process.

There were also times of great peace and benediction in the evenings when Krishna would recognize and welcome august beings whom he would see appear over the mountains and who would come to the room where Krishna and Helen and Nitya were. Krishna described them as majestic, noble, shining. Nitya and Helen only felt their presence, sensing pervasive power and blessing.

The sessions went on all summer, with Helen in attendance night after night, holding and soothing the body while it was undergoing excruciating pain. The girl kept a diary for those months, hoping an explanation might come for the strange happenings she witnessed.

There were other puzzling aspects to the months spent in Ehrwald. Their days were a mixture of high spiritual enlightenment and just plain tomfoolery. The latter was quite possibly a reaction to the intense holiness felt at other times. The group was often kiddish and frolicsome, with Krishna at moments turning from serious aloofness to wild and even silly behavior. He was often the ringleader in their practical jokery. Helen was astounded at his quick transitions.

He would also have serious sessions with Lady Emily's daughters and the other girls, in rotation. Helen and the others went solemnly to Krishna as they would go to a priest for confession. They voiced their problems and were sharply criticized for various of their attitudes or actions. He urged deep involvement in the moment's possibilities. He called for intense scrutiny of each passing incident.

He lamented that none of them were changing fundamentally. "If you love, feel great love. If you feel grief, let it rock you to the bottom." "Be immensely great in all you think and feel." "Change yourself and you will change the world." He usually berated them for their lack of purpose or their poor behavior: either they were not serious enough or they were too serious. There were always things he could accuse them of and usually the hour with him ended in their weeping. He seemed more satisfied when he had reduced them to tears; then he knew that he had touched them in their hearts.

He spoke often to them of fear—which meant little to Helen. She had no sense of fear at all and wondered why he brought it up so often. She had no fear of not being loved, no fear of death or of loneliness or of old age. Why all this talk of fear, she wondered.

His reprimands and injunctions were sharp and stern. He responded sarcastically to timorous questions, confessions, or human appeals. There was no coddling and there were no acceptable excuses. On hindsight, Helen could almost say that he seemed to take a fierce delight in stirring up their emotions. It was almost sadistic. She can remember no instance of any of the girls (including herself, the "enfant cherie" at the time) leaving their interviews with him shining and radiant and fulfilled.

He urged them to be themselves, not blind followers. He wanted them to strike out on their own, to look to the future when they would be adults in an adult world. He held up to the girls the models of Mrs. Besant and Dr. Mary Rocke, an old friend, as stalwart, strong, independent, impressive women for them to emulate.

Her close contact with Krishna during the Ehrwald summer helped Helen make up her mind that a possible musical career belonged to the past and that the future with him was more important by far. This would not entirely please her parents. They had hoped she would persevere and succeed with her music. They would have to be informed: she stood at the close of one cycle of experience and upon the threshold of another. After arguments with her parents by mail, during which they showed themselves to be firmly opposed to her giving up serious work on the violin, she decided to sail back to the United States. She would consult with her parents, informing them of her resolve, and then go on to join the group of young aspirants gathered at the Manor in Sydney, dedicating a life of service to the coming World Teacher.

An unhappy time resulted, as her parents disapproved of her new objectives. They insisted that she keep up with her violin. She wanted greatly to go on to Ojai to be part of Krishna's continuing process, and he wrote many sad letters, hoping she would come. Her father was adamantly against her going either to Ojai or Sydney, so she was trapped at home, feeling her time was wasted in trivial activities—torn between the new friends she loved so well and abiding by her father's dicta. A thoroughly unsatisfactory winter ensued at home with her family. She saw old friends and beaux and played the violin in local recitals and for neighborhood churches, but did not put her heart into her music as she had in Europe.

When Krishna and Nitya sailed for Europe from New York in the spring of 1924, Helen was on the boat with them, to the extreme disapproval of her father, who was brokenhearted at her decision. He left for his office that morning without a good-bye word and had no communication with her for years, until he wrote begging her to return so that he could see her "in the years of young womanhood."

That summer Helen was in Pergine, the north of Italy, with Krishna and Nitya and Lady Emily, her daughters Betty and Mary, and a few other of Krishna's friends. They rented a castle high on a hill overlooking the valley and village below. She and Lady Emily were in the square-tower end of the castle where Krishna and Nitya also lodged. The rest of the party were in the vast main building. Helen practiced her violin in the gloomy dungeon keep of the castle.

Krishna and Helen were together as much as they could be in such a crowded compass. Mary Lutyens says in her biography of Krishna that in Pergine, Krishna had begun to lose interest in Helen. That is hardly the feeling suggested by a remark he made to her as she entered his room in the tower one day: "I could drink the water from your body." Krishna's process continued with extreme pains but not as regularly as before. She attended him whenever she could, when he or Nitya signaled the need. She thought only of closeness and solace when she lay with him, holding him not as a lover but as a mother would.

Nearly every day Krishna gathered the group together and exhorted them to be exemplary and to achieve greatness in their lives. "Meet life directly," he urged. "Be extraordinarily alert, aware, all the time watching, open to every challenge, to every opportunity and hint." Here was beginning the decade of his life when inspired effusions poured forth from him in lyrical odes and prose, notably *The Hymn of the Initiate Triumphant*: "I have stood in Thy holy presence. I have seen the splendor of Thy face." And *The Road-Mender*: "There was a man mending a road: that man was myself, the pickaxe he held was myself, the very stone he was breaking was part of me, the tender blade of grass was my very being and the tree beside the man was myself."

It was a happy, ebullient time. Only Nitya's health disturbed them. His fund of energy was low, and he rarely participated in their volleyball games and expeditions. After an inspirational time in the Italian hill country the whole entourage sailed for Bombay on a liner from Trieste.

The first experiences of India were revelations for Helen: the sights, sounds, scents, and colors, the gentle dark people and their curious accents, the beautiful houses where she and her friends stayed, the street people in the surrounding poverty who were homeless beggars. She had never been in such beauty, such luxury, or seen such living conditions, both high and low. She was submerged in new sensations and observations, but she stayed in Bombay and the exotic milieu of Adyar, the International Theosophical Headquarters near Madras, only for a few weeks before being sent on to Australia by Krishna and Mrs. Besant.

There she lived the most flowerlike, felicitous time of her life. These were a happy, fulfilling two-and-a-half years; she was in her early twenties, living with other aspiring young people on a beautiful stretch of Sydney Harbor. She used her violin constantly, playing in churches and on the radio with a quartet. She learned to play the pipe organ and substituted for the regular organist. She typed and did secretarial work for Bishop Leadbeater—Brother, as the young people called him. She organized theatrics and small concerts for the others at the Manor. And of course she meditated and lived on a very exalted plane indeed, according to her opinions of the time. She was doing what Krishna advised; she was where he wanted her to be, and she was evolving spiritually as he had hoped.

Nitya's tuberculosis was worsening; his suffering increased. Advised to seek a better climate for him than India, the brothers decided on California where, for a time, Nitya's condition seemed to improve.

Nitya had always been an exemplification to Helen of the finest second fiddle who ever played. He had the competence to be first violinist and had a fine mind and was a good student, in contradistinction to Krishna who read few books. But he disclaimed his powers and was content to stay in the background and let his brother shine. Nitya had a kindliness, a warmhearted sympathy for his fellow beings.

Krishna was gracious and polite, and was loving at some times, but extremely forbidding at others. His standards were mercilessly high. He was a flashing star, hardly human. Nitya was tremendously human. Helen felt the difference between the two brothers even when she was "enfant cherie" and "Krishna's girl." In the early days at Amsteldyk, when Krishna had showed her a photograph of Nitya, while he was less handsome than Krishna, she had felt an immediate rapport. Alas, he died too soon and was unable to fulfill his brilliant prospects.

In December of 1925 Krishna and Helen met again in Adyar when a contingent from Sydney went to India for an international convention. Krishna had sailed there from America leaving Nitya behind in California. Nearing Bombay on November 14, Krishna received a cable on the boat notifying him that Nitya had died the previous day from influenza after his long bout of tuberculosis. The shock was great—so great that it cut life out from under Krishna's feet. To Helen he wrote: "Ever since Nitya has gone away the sunsets, the trees & the stars are not the same. Something has gone which can never again, in this life, come back." And later in his journal he wrote: "There was no movement in any direction away from sorrow."

He arrived in Adyar a changed person—older, colder, more restrained. The boy in him was gone. There was affection between Helen and Krishna as heretofore and she spent every afternoon with him on his top floor veranda overlooking the beautiful Adyar River, but the loss of his brother killed something in him. He now knew that he would be without close kin for the rest of his life. Something inside him turned to steel.

A personal love life began to become peripheral to Krishna's burgeoning public life and public image after Helen returned to Sydney. The link between them was lessening. Letters no longer flew constantly from him to her. There had begun to be differences between them. New influences and people came into his life in India, England, and America, and new ones were coming into hers.

She was developing a mind of her own and encountering the socialist movement in Australia. She went to meetings and visited slums in Sydney with socialist friends. She remembered the vast abyss she had seen between the ultrarich in India and the homeless who slept in the streets and alleys and gutters of Bombay and Calcutta while he and she and Krishna's friends slept comfortably in rich homes. She no longer lived in the circles in which Krishna moved in London and India. He consorted with top people and rarely if ever stayed in humble or poor homes or hotels. He was surrounded by the well-to-do and the famous and influential. This gave her cause for thought.

Krishna was certainly not a social reformer and was far removed ideologically and physically from the masses. His message to the world was that change must come from within the individual and not through political action and economic reforms from the outside, enforced from above. Only through inner change of the individual could the world be permanently affected or transformed. He thought Gandhi's preoccupation with political issues, with racial segregation and economic exploitation, was misplaced. He even condemned Gandhi as a "very violent man" on the wrong path in trying to change the world through class struggle.

It was in the soul of humanity that changes would be made, Krishna propounded. He seemed to think that anyone, anywhere, anytime, in any situation, could reach the pinnacle of life experience and being, and need not be affected by status or circumstances. In his opinion, outer conditions, extreme poverty, lack of opportunity and education could all be surmounted by the mind.

A total all-round relationship was never really achieved between Helen and Krishna. Perhaps they had not had time enough together to grow together. They were in each other's company during six years not more than a few months in all. His letters and hers in return located their love only on paper. "To make love a matter of affectional letterwriting merely is like trying to paint a picture without the use of pigments. In this way a quite complete relation is seldom realized. For any big and permanent relationship there has to be a rather gradual and slow accumulation," wrote Edward Carpenter in *Drama of Life and Death*. On reading Krishna's missives now, Helen opines he was half in love with love itself instead of with her.

Helen never knew quite when and why he lost interest in her and severed connections: whether it was a gradual letting go, or a considered decision to dispense with her when there was no longer the need—or when someone else took her place. It happened toward the end of her stay in Sydney or soon after the return to the United States. It is possible or even probable that he was put off by a news story which appeared in Indian and American papers that Krishnamurti was said to be engaged to marry a young American girl. Helen believed that he had been advised by older, wiser heads in America and England to deny the story (and rightly so, for it was not true), and also to cut off, or at least to lessen, a relationship which could interfere with his mission.

Helen had been there when he needed her, or needed someone. In any case, what was there so powerful for him to be in love with? Even then she knew that while she had high aspirations, she was lower on the scale of livingness. She had no magnificent talent, no overwhelming beauty or distinction, no great intellect, no fame, no monetary contribution to make. He was a star performer. The famous and well-to-do of both sexes orchestrated his life.

If love is a complex mix of human relations, Helen and Krishna did not experience the elements of physical and mental growth together that would have caused their relationship to flourish. They had in some degree only the emotional and spiritual elements. This, with continents and seas between them, was not enough food for love. Krishna once bubbled with a new and novel emotion. She responded at a budding level. What could it have come to?

Considering the pages-long avowals of the past, the last letter she kept of his could hardly have been more flat or cursory. He passed through New York City en route to Europe without seeing her in her nearby hometown.

Sarobia, Eddington, Pa.
June 11, 1936

My Dear Helen:

Thank you very much for your letter. I shall be in New York till before the 28th or so. We can arrange to see each other before the 18th. I hope this will be convenient to you. I hope you don't mind if I don't write much as I have a lot to do.

With love,

Krishna

[Here I return to first person.]

Did I laugh or sigh over this laconic brush-off? Today it seems hilarious after all the fervent protestations of his earlier letters:

"Darling Helen, please, please, I beg of you believe me in all this that I have written, and don't ever doubt my love or my devotion to yourself, I beg of you. All this ardor and what one might call infatuation are perfectly true and lasting and so is my devotion for you. Remember that, darling. Do write and tell me that you haven't completely forgotten Krishna. I wonder how long you will remember me or like me!" (Of course, it was he who forgot me in later years.)

"I greatly hope that your father will still remain in the T.S. and you, too, Helen dear. It would be rather amusing if you left the T.S. and refused to see Krishna again. By Jove, that would be a good joke. Anyway, I hope it will never come true." (But it was Krishna who left the Theosophical Society and he who would not see me.)

"You, my beloved, will always be with me, whatever I am doing & whatever I am thinking. Anyway, forget me or do anything you like, I shall love my Helen. I wonder if a time will come when you will say, 'I remember very vaguely that name. I seem to know him. What is that Krishna, anyway?' I hope that will never happen." (But it did happen, to him, not me.)

Years later, when I was in India on my own, staying in Madras at the home of my friend Vishy, Rajkumar of Viziana-gram, I wrote to Krishna who was giving talks in Madras, saying that after all those years I would like to see him again for old time's sake. The answer to my note was not: "My dear Helen, what a pleasant surprise to be able to see you again. Come for lunch." Instead, I received an official telephone call from his secretary: "Mr. Krishnamurti can see you at 3:00 P.M., Wednesday the twenty-fourth."

I entered the room at the appointed time, being one of a half-dozen people awaiting their appointments. Well I knew how that had been years before when I, however, had not had to wait in line. Eventually, I was ushered into a room with two straight chairs facing each other. We shook hands formally, Krishna saying, "How do you do?" To make conversation, he asked politely, "And is this your first trip to India?" I might have answered, "I came the first time practically in your arms," but laughed and said I had been there before with Lady Emily and so on. He hastily said, "Of course, of course," and then we chatted together a bit. The conversation was inconsequential and soon my allotted time was up.

The next in line was a lovely Hindu woman, a musician with whom I had talked about an upcoming concert to which I had been invited there and then. This new acquaintance was warmer and more cordial than the distant man who had once vowed he would love me forever and who now paced up and down waiting impatiently for the next client. Not a flicker even of friendliness was left. He had no more care for me or interest than he had for the fly on the wall.

There are those among his followers who say that the deliberate cutting off of the past was an essential part of his teachings, part of his mission: You are not supposed to judge Krishnamurti's behavior by ordinary standards; he was a higher form of being; he was unique and not as others are. All the more reason, I think, why one might expect higher standards of behavior.

Could not kindliness and consideration and love also have been part of his mission? I could enumerate a dozen or more loyal devotees of both sexes, and long-term friends of his, who were dropped by him in later years. I doubt that his brother would have repudiated old friendships and loyalties. I know that Nitya was deeply disturbed at his brother's turning his back on the Theosophical Society and rejecting the teachings and former kindnesses of its leaders.

Krishnamurti was like other human beings—the sum of his memories and experiences. How could he completely disown them? If none of those people he came to know had existed, what would he have been? He himself said in one of his dialogues at Saanen in Switzerland in the 1960s, "We cannot live without memories. If you had no memory at all you would be in a state of amnesia and wouldn't know what you were doing, your name or where you lived. Memory obviously has a place." Yet he could say another time: "Memory is not necessary. I am not locked into the past. . . . Memories are ashes of everything dead and buried." He has been quoted as saying in a discussion in India: "There is never a sense of coming back to a relation. There are no anchorages: there is simply a moving on."

I could and did understand that. Life flows and changes. Earlier friendships or loves are not necessarily lasting. But I agree with and respond totally to Aldous Huxley's charmingly simple confession: "It is a little embarrassing that, after forty-five years of research and study, the best advice I can give to people is to be a little kinder to each other."

Did Krishna like his audiences? Did he need to be so peremptory with them? These were my thoughts not only when I was on the outside looking in, but even when I was one of the chosen inner circle. In answering questions, he sometimes showed irritation and disdain bordering on arrogance. Earnest inquiries were brushed aside roughly. After a prolonged talk on love and detachment, I watched him completely demolish an abashed questioner. Could he not put himself in another person's shoes?

The poetic phase of Krishna's self-expression which first manifested in Pergine in 1924 did not carry on into his later life, at least not in his public utterances, which were cooly abstract, although in his private diaries and notebooks he continued to reveal his more lyrical side: "I have drunk at the source and long to bring everyone to it." A state of rapture and spontaneous ecstasy sometimes came in floods in his notebooks, such as when he recorded his waking thoughts and his strolls through nature over the course of some months in 1961. These passages were beautifully written, eloquently expressing his highest states of consciousness.

The bald prosaic facts I tell of his everyday self are picayune beside the wondrous emotions he depicts in those almost daily effusions. The benediction and complete immersion in nature he touched then went far beyond personal emotion or sentiment. These writings show the finest part of his being, far from the cold platform demeanor and the high disdain that could emanate from him at other times. Here his inner being overshadowed his lesser side, which had its foibles, its likes and dislikes.

From my last Madras encounter I never spoke with him again personally, although if I were in a city where he might be speaking I went to hear him talk, to see in what direction his mind was working. Like a winter sun, in his lectures there no longer seemed to be warmth—just intellectualizing that did not fit my earlier idealization of him.

He seemed to exist to talk. He decried teachers and teaching and claimed to have a horror of authority, but he occupied authoritarian platforms all over the world and spoke endlessly to uncountable thousands as a teacher. He tirelessly devoted the greater part of his life to traveling around the world giving, whenever and wherever he could, his message of living in the eternal present; of being intensely aware every moment; of seeking quality in living; of dropping petty aims; and of self-transformation through inner realization, not through any organization, ritual, or creed.

Reaching his thirties, he had rejected the title of guru and the role prepared for him, preferring to be known simply as a philosopher and speaker. Why did he resist and refuse the title of World Teacher? He spent his whole life teaching. Are teachers absolutely necessary when we want to learn the piano, for instance? Perhaps not. But by profiting from their greater knowledge, guidance, and experience, one can at least be saved a great deal of trouble and time. What if somebody alleged to be the World Piano Teacher came and told us that all piano professors were only so many obstacles to our ever learning how to play the piano?

Philip Wylie wrote in *The Magic Animal*: "What the world needs is a new sort of iconoclast, a man who will set about smashing all of the temples, cathedrals, churches, synagogues, and holy structures, but who will do it without the aim of setting upon the ruin a new edifice for new gods as the sign of his new doctrine."

Might Krishnamurti have been this man? Was he not an iconoclast and image-breaker? Had he not done his best to tear down what he considered to be false beliefs? The Theosophical Society, which had given him his start in life, underwent staggering losses in membership due to his teaching that devotees should abandon all organizations.

Krishna claimed to live an "unconditioned" life, in complete detachment and freedom from circumstances and from obligations. This was what he expounded and how he professed to live. Yet he was surrounded and supported by worldly friends. He lived a padded though dedicated life. Who is "unconditioned" in this physical world? Certainly not the Krishnamurti who slept in comfortable beds in costly houses, who got up in the morning, gargled, abluted, combed his hair, and dressed in fine clothes bought in elegant shops. He had to eat like the rest of us; he got sick and was nursed, spent his time with so-and-so and chose to do such-and-such. He was conditioned and affected every second of his life, just as everyone else was and is.

Krishna stayed in the most distinguished homes and expensive hotels. When I asked him, "Why never in a YMCA or some humble home?" he would say, "But Helen, they never ask. I go where I am invited." I knew the poorer sort would never dare to ask. When, later in our lives, I invited him to Forest Farm in Vermont, where, as I told him in advance, we lived simply with no electricity, with only a pump in the kitchen for water and an outhouse in the woods, and where I would meet him in a pickup truck, he chose instead to go to a lovely home in Pennsylvania where he could be with his own kind.

From the time he was discovered he lived very upper class and adopted his benefactors' high-toned accents, their clothing, their manners. True, he took care of his own elegant suits, keeping them in condition for years, and he polished his shoes to brilliant brightness. He loved fine cars, keeping them immaculately clean. True, he spoke kindly and politely to servitors and menials, and in his early days at Arya Vihara in Ojai, he worked around the place in grubby clothes at times, but on the whole he knew little of physical work and had little or no contact with poor people. Few if any workers attended his talks; he had little appeal for the masses.

He admired people who were successful, brainy, presentable, and talented. He cohorted with famous names. He had achieved so much in his own life and felt comfortable with other greats. It would perhaps be fair to say (and not invidiously) that he was first class in everything. That was clear to me and completely admissable; he *was* a first class person. Yet so were Mother Theresa and Gandhi and Schweitzer, who spent their entire lives with the poor and downtrodden.

Krishna's character and being remain a mystery to me to this day. I am grateful for the opportunity to have been close to him for a time. I am glad of the association and appreciative of the opportunity for loving and for being loved. It was a rare happening I would not have wanted to miss. It was also an edifying entrance into the stark realities of human relationships.

The top of the tree does not always remain the top of the tree. Other branches grow higher and higher. Blossoms appear where none were before. I had had halcyon years with Krishna. Let others take my place. Let others get and give something of what I had given and received.

Krishna had many women friends after I passed out of the picture. I heard of them and knew some of them personally. How passionately he became attached to them I did not know nor really care. I hoped the relationships were fond and productive of good on both sides.

My own togetherness with him had been rare, pure, and chaste. We both were amazingly virginal in thought and deed. We loved, but seemingly did not need the physical. An idealistic tenderness was the ultimate relationship we dreamt or thought of. "It is curious," wrote Edward Carpenter, "how falling in love paralyzes for a time, inhibiting the mental part and even the physical." In one of Krishna's letters to me he wrote, "My dearest Helen, good afternoon. I kiss your hand, if I am permitted. But otherwise, I merely bow, very low down."

In time Krishna no longer needed nor wanted me. I did not make the first move, nor did I make the last. I served where possible when I was wanted and retired when the need was no longer expressed. Krishna moved on and I moved on—in different directions. Surprisingly philosophical and unpossessive, I went back to Ridgewood and our letters to each other dwindled and then stopped. I slid back to a more mundane scale and tempo, while he ascended to a more dramatic role.

Were Krishnamurti's teachings wasted on me? Was I not up to comprehending his message? Had I failed to mature along with him? That is what his later followers might think. Yet if not assimilated in one way, his influence worked on me in other ways. I probably digested as much as I was ready for, and much of the rest became part of my being in time.

Krishna had said each person must liberate her- or himself and strike out on her or his own path. And so I did, without too much delay. The interval I spent in New Jersey, at home again after years in Europe and Australia was not easy. I had grown away from childhood friends and found no new ones locally. Suburban life no longer appealed. I practiced my violin and played publicly on various occasions. But it was an empty, untenanted waiting period in my life. What was in the wings? The best thing that could have happened to me: I met Scott Nearing through a fortuitous phone call. Our relationship was a far healthier one. We started slowly, sanely, and surely, building up gradually, step-by-step, and stayed together for over half a century.

Both of Us Together

You and I have found the secret way,
None can bar our love or say us nay:
All the world may stare and never know
You and I are twined together so.

. . .

You and I have laughed the leagues apart
In the soft delight of heart to heart.
If there's a gulf to meet or limit set,
You and I have never found it yet.

A. E., "The Secret Love"

SCOTT NEARING WAS forty-five when we met the second time, in 1928. He was in the midpart of his turbulent life, and at the nadir of his heretofore brilliant career. He had proven his abilities as a teacher, author, and orator. I in my midtwenties was ingenuous, untried, and easygoing, far from his academic competencies and experience. Although an ardent, almost immoderate reader from early childhood, I had only a high school education behind me.

Scott had dedicated himself to promoting the general welfare of his fellow citizens and country, yet he had been thrown out of academia and was socially and politically ostracized, his career in ruins. He was a social leper, alone and outcast even from his family, when I entered his life. Protected, carefree, nonchalant, I had known no other discipline aside from my years of application to music and was largely ignorant of the practical and political world in which Scott was preeminent.

My bourgeois background of dilettante musicianship hardly prepared me for an attachment to this rugged and determined radical—or for him to see anything in me.

Nigel Nicolson wrote about his parents Vita Sackville-West and Harold Nicolson in his book *Portrait of a Marriage*: "Men and women who marry ought to be positive and negative—complementary elements." I knew that Scott and I were vastly dissimilar—he with his extreme erudition, with his precise and well-trained mind; and me so fanciful, wayward, with next to no schooling—but we shared subtle as yet undefined ties. In him the left side of the brain, the logical and consecutive, predominated; in me it was the right side, the imaginative, the experimental, the novel.

A psychologically insightful person wrote to us later in our lives: "You are true opposites and perfectly complement one another. What each may have lacked in the beginning the other one had. Now your qualities are integrated equally." An adept astrologer, seeing our lion and fish signs, foretold an "unusually strange attraction between the two. It might give a sort of spiritual, fairy-story kind of enchantment, something not of this earth."

For those interested in astrology (and even deriders often know their birth signs), here are summaries of the horoscopes of our two personalities:

"Helen Knothe was born at 7:08 A.M., February 23, 1904, in the sign of Pisces, with the sun rising 3° in the 12th house, denoting paramount interest in things occult, with Mercury and Saturn also in the 12th house adding emphasis to that leaning. Venus was in her house of friends (the 11th) which is favorable, with the moon in Taurus in the 2nd house giving stability and sturdiness to an otherwise dreamy and visionary character. Uranus in midheaven in the 10th house in direct opposition to Neptune in the 4th house makes her strongly independent if not eccentric and reckless, and at variance with her family. Mars and Jupiter in conjunction in Aries, her 1st house, give some spunk and physical vigor to an otherwise weird and dreamy double Pisces character. She is bound to be unconventional, impulsive, independent, and likely to make her own small mark in a larger world."

"Scott Nearing was born at 11:00 A.M., August 6, 1883, in Morris Run, Tioga County, Pennsylvania, in the sign of Leo. His planets were all above the horizon, and most of them directly in midheaven. With this striking setup he was a born leader and could have been president. The sign Libra was rising, giving emphasis to the determination to bring justice and balance to the consciousness of his time. The beneficent triangle formed between his Libra ascendant and Mars, Saturn, and Pluto in Gemini's 8th house offered him an opportunity to delve into dark and hidden matters with tenacity and to publicly express his findings with eloquence. Moon conjunction Uranus in Virgo gave him the tendency for extreme order in all things. In the midheaven, symbolic of the public interests, one finds Jupiter in Cancer, with Venus, Sun, and Mercury in Leo. All of these together create a forceful personality who will work to use his influence for the good of humanity at large."

Jung has written: "The meeting of two personalities is like the contact of two chemical substances—if there is any reaction, both are transformed." And so it was with us.

Our first moves were not so much toward being lovers as toward being friends, to explore and learn from each other. Scott had much to teach me from his wider experience of life and the "real" world. He was conscientious and careful, if not conservative, in his work—whether it was at his desk, in the garden or woods, or driving a car. I, on my part, was untrained, extremely fanciful, and capricious. I took up sporadic and varied enthusiasms, dabbling in astrology, palmistry, and graphol-ogy, and was an amateur, not particularly proficient in anything. Only in music did I surpass him.

He was a scheduled person, always on time, with so many considered hours for this and so many hours for that occupa-tion. Given my helter-skelter background, it was strange how I appreciated his regimes and fitted in with little trouble, though I never learned to fold my clothes neatly at bedtime as he did, but flung them off in any direction under his amazed and amused gaze. "I bet you even fold up your toilet paper neat and square," I once mockingly accused him, and he acknowledged that he did.

Let's say I gave him comfort and company in his isolation from the academic world. My melodies were not always up to his emphatic solo but I sang in tune with him, and we moved to the same tempos. Together somehow we harmonized, I ad-justing to his tune as he did to mine. My talents were minor, his major, but our lives together revealed new chords, new and unexpected fugues in our lifetime duet.

One of the most touching things he ever wrote to me was his dedication in his autobiography: "To Helen, who did half the work." That justified my existence to myself.

To bring him along my path, I introduced him to my love—music. This was a new world for him. My hundreds of classical phonograph records ranged from Bach to Brahms to Bartok and I induced him to listen. He came to appreciate the limpid tones of Kathleen Ferrier's deep contralto voice, the ex-pressive lieder singer Dietrich Fischer-Dieskau, the "War" sym-phonies of Benjamin Britten and Shostakovich, and Vaughan Williams's "Antarctica." Atonal modern music and rock he found merely "poundy" and "noisy." And he could not under-stand why Beethoven's symphonies were played by everyone over and over again. "You've heard them and know them; why not go on to other music? Why not make your own?"

I did teach him how to play the recorder and he sometimes took it with him on lecture trips. I liked to think of him in lonely hotel rooms fumbling with his large fingers practicing in preparation for our simple flute duets. Among the few times I ever saw him very angry was once when, disgusted with his ineptitude and false notes, he threatened to throw the instrument into the fire.

In a book on Russia which I came across, it was noted that "Lenin was by no means a lover of music. Like so many Russian intellectuals, he felt that music should be followed immediately by the action it inspired. 'We must not stay longer,' he said once to Maxim Gorky as he led him away from the concert they were attending. 'This music makes me soft.'"

Scott found arranged, dressed-up concerts too formal and constrained. I took him to such affairs and he went, but reluctantly. When he ignominiously slept (and snored) through a wondrous Metropolitan performance of "Pelleas and Melisande," I pulled him out and vowed, "Never again an opera."

I was often queried by my friends of earlier years, "How can you, so artistic, and with such a musical and even mystical background, spend your life with such a man—a pedant, a communist, an austere chap who knows so little about music and art? He will change you and dominate you, take all the lilt out of you. You will lose your individuality which we so prize. You are wasting yourself and your talents."

I always replied by saying that no art could compare with life, that Scott's art was in his living. I stoutly maintained that Scott was the finest person I had ever met, that I was thoroughly happy living with him and could choose no better mate. To live with an older, wiser man who could answer all my questions was a continual delight; it was school and holiday all in one. I had a supportive, understanding teacher, one tolerant of my many idiosyncrasies. "Anybody can have a husband, but to few is it given to have a sage, and the combination of both is as rare as it is useful," I quoted from the anonymously written *Elizabeth and Her German Garden.*

As to his roughness and toughness, Edna Ferber has a scene in *So Big* in which the heroine refuses a suitor. "Some day," she says, "I'll probably marry a horny-handed son of toil, and if I do it will be the horny hands that will win me. If you want to know, I like 'em with their scars on them. There's something about a man who has fought for it, a look in his eyes, the feel of his hand. He needn't have been successful—though he probably would be. . . . *You* haven't a mark on you. Not a mark. If you had kept on fighting and struggling and sticking it out—why, that fight would show in your face today—in your eyes and your jaw and your hands and in your way of standing and walking and sitting and talking. You're all smooth. I like 'em bumpy."

Artistry can also be in the honesty of one's lifestyle, in one's order, in one's character. Havelock Ellis wrote: "The true artist is not one who draws or paints, but rather that person whose whole life is adjusted to beauty in every thought and action." Scott was an artist in his neat and tidy, thriving vegetable gardens, in his straight wood and compost piles, in his brightly shining tools, in his meticulous notebooks, in his careful, legible script. I felt he made his very life a work of art.

The public knew the tough, pedantic side of Scott, his stubbornness on matters of principle. To me he showed an unpredictable, light, and perceptive side of his nature. We had our yeasty moments together. A friend glancing out of her window one day in Connecticut saw us running along the top of a stone wall, I in advance and Scott agilely following. And one warm spring day we had been skiing in shorts on an isolated hill on the Fern Pass in Tirolese Austria. I proposed taking off everything, so, nude, we sped down the slopes wearing only big ski boots and skis. What a sight that would have been for onlookers, but no one was around. Before Cape Rosier became too inhabited we never wore bathing suits; Scott was a good swimmer and we often enjoyed the cold sea water of Spirit Cove in front of our house in Maine. He taught me a delightful trick in the salt water: sitting upright with legs straight out ahead and paddling about, floating as if in a boat, just enjoying the slight motion and the sun and the air.

We often slept out in the fields or woods when on short trips in his small two-seater Ford, a Flivver. We bought thirteen-dollar sleeping bags and camped out on many a night. The hard ground, open air, and nighttime skies became part of our pleasure together. In *Travels with a Donkey in the Cévennes* Robert Louis Stevenson wrote: "And yet even while I was exulting in my solitude I became aware of a strange lack. I wished a companion to lie near me in the starlight, silent and not moving, but ever within touch. For there is a fellowship more quiet even than solitude, and which, rightly understood, is solitude made perfect. To live out of doors with the woman a man loves [or the man a woman loves] is of all lives the most complete and free."

Early on, in his enforced isolation from his academic peers, this intimacy with a young, politically illiterate girl must have been a break in Scott's usual patterns. His life was in transition; here were pastel colors introduced into a lonely and perhaps somber existence.

His discernment of my peculiar character was shown when he saw me off on one of my European trips in the 1930s. He brought to the boat a twenty-cent tin flute he had picked up

Helen, age four, standing next to mother, Maria, with sister, Alice,
brother, Alex, and father, Frank Knothe, 1908.

Helen as a junior high school student in Ridgewood,
New Jersey, 1920.

Helen with Krishnamurti in Ommen, Holland, 1921.

Helen with Rapagopal on the left and Krishnamurti and Nityananda on the right in Ehrwald, Austria, 1923.

Helen on the far left with Nityananda on the right and other members of the summer group in Pergine, Italy, 1924.

Krishanmurti, 1924.

Helen, 1924.

Helen with Scott on her first trip to the USSR, 1931.

Helen at Forest Farm in Vermont, March 1947.

Helen and Scott playing flute outside their stone house at Forest Farm in Vermont, 1950. *Photo by Rebecca Lepkoff*

Helen stoking the five-by-fifteen-foot evaporator for making maple sugar
at Forest Farm, Vermont, 1950.

Helen and Scott on the stone patio at Forest Farm, Vermont, 1951.
Photo by Irene Strauss

Helen building the stone wall around the garden in Maine, late 1960s.
Photo by Richard Garrett

Visitors eating lunch at the Nearing's farm in Maine, mid-1970s.

View of the farm house and garden, Maine, mid-1970s.
Photo by Richard Garrett

Helen and Scott seated next to the original frame house, Maine, 1978.
Photo by Lotte Jacobi

Helen and Scott working on the stone wall, Maine, late 1970s.
Photo by Ralph T. Gardner

Helen and Scott seated by the window looking out over Penobscot
Bay, Maine, 1978. *Photo by Ralph T. Gardner*

Scott standing next to the stone house, Maine, 1979. *Photo by Ken Williams*

Helen and Scott sawing wood, Maine, 1980. *Photo by Glynne Robinson Betts*

Helen and Scott seated by their stone house, Maine, 1982.
Photo by Jennifer Cannell

from a street peddler and a large wholesale box of huge, black Bing cherries. I was to consume the cherries (a great favorite of mine) and spit out the pits as I walked the deck; the flute was to tootle in my cabin on seasick days. Another chap would have brought a mere pound or two of cherries, or a box of chocolates, or a bunch of roses. A flute and loads of cherries were more my style. That little tin flute started out my interest in flute playing. In Rotterdam when the ship landed I bought a fine Cocobola recorder; so it was at his instigation that I added another facet to my love of music.

Another quite sentimental side of Scott shows in a Robert Service poem he typed out and sent to me in Europe.

> I know a garden where the lilies gleam,
>   And one who lingers in the sunshine there;
>   She is than white-stoled lily far more fair,
> And oh, her eyes are heaven-lit with dream!
>
> I know a garret, cold and dark and drear,
>   And one who toils and toils with tireless pen,
>   Until his brave, sad eyes grow weary—then
> He seeks the stars, pale, silent as a seer.
>
> And ah, it's strange; for, desolate and dim,
>   Between these two there rolls an ocean wide;
>   Yet he is in the garden by her side
> And she is in the garret there with him.

I found a more unconventional one by Countee Cullen to return to him.

> "Live like the wind," he said, "unfettered,
>   And love me while you can;
> And when you will, and can be bettered,
>   Go to the better man.

"For you'll grow weary, maybe, sleeping
   So long a time with me;
Like this there'll be no cause for weeping;
   The wind is always free.

"Go when you please," he would be saying,
   His mouth hard on her own;
That's why she stayed and loved the staying,
   Contented to the bone.

One aspect of Scott was stern and didactic, unyielding as to right and wrong. The other was affable, kind, friendly, and, as his choice of poetry shows, even romantic. Luckily I came in under the warm umbrella of his loving side, though sometimes he tried to yank me towards his extreme rectitude.

Here is one of his first long letters, admonishing and instructing me:

> How do you make a day that feels like a harmonious unity instead of a chaos? Abstractly it is the problem that every human faces: how to live with the least loss and the greatest increments of growth. (Ordinarily this is stated: how to live with the least pain and the most pleasure.)
>
> This problem can be analyzed as follows:
>
> 1. Establishing a center of interest, a nucleus from which to "take off" in the daily living process.
>
> 2. Contact with the cosmos; with the unseen, unfolding, eternal forces of which each individual is a part and with which each is more or less in contact.
>
> 3. Finding some form of work (creative activity) into which the individual can concentrate his being; into which he can go with his whole heart. This may or may not be the source of his livelihood.

4. Establishing satisfactory and more or less permanent social contacts; friendships; personal relations.

5. Gradually knitting together a unified, integrated, poised personality that is constantly expanding (growing).

He followed this letter with a short note. "You will doubtless say to yourself: 'The scoundrel is trying to reform me.' Wrong, my dear. How many times have I told you I want you as you are? You come closer to me, in more ways, than any other person in the world. Why should I want you changed? Even if I could reform you, I wouldn't dare. I might botch the job."

When I reread his old letters now, I wonder what my responses may have been, but none of my letters remain. He had kept no correspondence since that time during the First World War when his Toledo, Ohio, home was entered by government agents and searched, and unopened letters as well as other mail and papers were appropriated.

As part of my early education, he wrote concerning a query of mine about joining some liberal woman's organization:

Social reform activities are likely to be divided into those which aim to modify the established order without changing its fundamental characteristics (i.e.—making war more humane; making poverty more tolerable; making the stockyards cleaner) and those which aim at basic changes (eliminating war; abolishing poverty; ceasing all forms of slaughter). People of a liberal turn of mind—and usually with some degree of comfort—dabble in the former (and sometimes work very hard at them), but since they are enjoying comfort under the established order, they do not try to change it very much.

You see, I usually push such questions back to an economic source. That is why Christian Science, Theosophy, etc. are so outwardly repugnant to me. I am wary of them. Those who profess such are usually part of the exploiting classes and live more or less comfortably off war and exploitation.

That leads me to one other comment—the book you sent me, *Conquest of Illusion*, by your friend Koos van der Leeuw. Thank you for letting me see it, and will you keep me in touch with other things of that kind. I am greatly interested in this line of thought. I have read a great deal of it in the past, and, since you are also interested, I have a double reason for wanting to know more.

Also keep me in touch with what Krishnamurti says and does. If he is a World Teacher, I want to know it.

Scott wrote me early on in our friendship:

When I get back from my trip, I wish you would review the past two months in light of this question: How much have you been able to get out of this period? I would like to hear you analyze the results of this kind of work for you. It is my belief that if you will stick around for a couple of years, maybe three or four, and work at things carefully and wisely, you can get a good training. First and simplest, a secretarial training, including typing, stenography; second, at least two foreign languages; third, training in research; and fourth, an insight into Social Science.

If you will turn over in your mind this question: What you have learned and how you have reacted to the past two months, we can plan the next months more intelligently. While you do stick around you will be compelled to put up with my queer ways, etc., but if you can endure that, the educational end of the proposition should prove well worthwhile. Let's talk things over, anyway, and make it as worthwhile as we possibly can.

Here are excerpts from several letters Scott wrote me in the first years of our association. The pages I kept are mostly undated.

We must work things out so that both of us lead rewarding lives and pass around to others some of the things we have learned. I believe we are uniquely situated to do this and I for one will do my utmost to make the possible come true. To be successful, both of us must make a contribution and both must make adjustments. I love you and trust you and believe, profoundly, in your immediately realizable potential of a full, rewarding and helpful life. Let's both go at it, and together. Life's best to you always.

Another:

I wish you well and join you in facing and meeting life. I feel as though we were beginning our working and living together. There seems to be something big about the idea. I know that you have been doing your share, and I have a feeling yours has been doing a bit for me. I shall creep into paradise in the shadow of your good works. Only last night I was thinking we had developed the technique of getting on together. I was never so close to anyone else. And I never thought that it would be possible to be so close. Our whole relationship has been a revelation to me, and a very real and great joy.

Again:

I am convinced that there are several important things we must do together. Let's inquire till we find out what they are and then let's set about the tasks. It is such a great joy to look forward to work with you. You are part of my life every hour and every day. I live in part through you. The ties that hold us together are many, and are very strong, and they mean so very much to me. Now and always I am willing that you should go when you are ready. But your staying is so great a joy to me, and if you go you will take a big part of my life with you.

A further note:

Often I feel that my personality stands in the way of your advancement. If that were so, it would be unfortunate beyond words. We both have our lives to live and our work to do. When we can live them and do our work together, that is very fine. But we must be careful not to stand in each other's way. We cannot over-emphasize the importance of this. We should have it constantly in mind. It is so clear to me this morning that I cannot possess you, nor you possess me—that we must both develop and use our own tools, but that we can work together.

You are a darling and I love you. You are as free to go as ever you were, but I do hope you stick around. I do not want to stand in the way of your development. I would like, on the contrary, to help you forward in every possible way. Friendship should mean that, and I am more than anxious to be your true friend. If the time ever comes when you feel that I am hindering your further progress, by all means say so and step out on your own account.

Within a year of our acquaintance, radical changes in my life were underway. I left the comfortable family home and rented a room for eleven dollars a week in downtown New York City. At Scott's suggestion, in order to experience life in the raw, I worked the whole winter of 1928–29 at various factory jobs: a paper mill, a box factory, and a candy packery. With wages between thirteen and fourteen dollars a week and with little left over for food, I remember living largely on grapefruit and Triscuits, and nibbling on stray chocolates that dropped off the moving belt of the machine.

Occasional dates with former swains who came to the factory gates to meet me (in their Cadillacs and Lincolns) were explained to my fellow workers: "He's just the shofer." I was called "Ellen, the German girl," because I spoke differently from the rest. Scoffing at my awkward handling of a broom under the machines, they jeered, "Looks as though she's never used a broom before." Little did they know that I never had.

All this while I was living alone and had not definitely or permanently tied up with Scott. He wrote me: "As I view it now, the winter has given you a very great deal. Perhaps best of all it has given a sense of direction and purpose within yourself. This you need, and this you seem now to have. If you have gained nothing else, the time has been well spent."

In the spring of 1929 Scott made the further suggestion that I might think of going back to my fancy European friends for a while to see which way of life I wanted to live, with him (the low life) or with them (the high life). I packed my bags, took the boat again for my beloved Holland (third class, this time, not as with my mother, first class) and was welcomed and feted and proposed to. It was easy to slip back into the carefree existence of the rich, in Paris, London, Amsterdam. Without Scott's influence I might have taken the easy way and married a title or a country house with a moat around it (this tempted me more than the title).

Then came a cable from Scott: "Enough cash granted to begin work on my book *War*. Will you come back and help?" I could not resist him or the opportunity to do some serious work. I quit suitors and the high life, cut off my long hair, distributed my best clothes and jewelry and fancy belongings to girlfriends, and made ready to go. I left my violin with my parents who were in Holland at the time. They had greatly hoped for an advantageous marriage and were not happy with my decision, but off I sailed on the next available steamer, knowing full well that this was another turning point in my life.

After a quiet reacquaintance week in the Green Mountains at a friend's secluded cabin, Scott and I rented a cheap room in Greenwich Village on West Eleventh Street and started living and working together. We did research daily in the New York

Public Library on Fifth Avenue and typing at home. I had found a trustworthy keel and he a sail for his boat. He had been reconciled to going on alone, tackling his life by himself, but was delighted to have acquired this willing helper. The nineteenth century American writer and editor Elbert Hubbard wrote: "Health, Books, and Work, with Love added, are a solace for all the stings and arrows of outrageous fortune."

So I became Scott's secretarial assistant as well as enlivening his life and opening him up to subjects he had barely tapped. Politically and practically he was the leader; in the more intangible artistic and spiritual domain I was the guide. We partook of each other's competencies. It became, as Edward Carpenter has expressed it, "an interchange of essences."

Our individual lives became intertwined. Though stronger and older, he did not tend to dominate. Each of us brought something new to the relationship. Our diverse interests became mutual; our separated concerns became common. Constant meetings and companionship deepened our appreciation of the unique individuality each was to the other, and we grew into a living side-by-side that was warm and fulfilling. Antoine de Saint-Exupéry wrote: "Love does not consist in gazing at each other, but in looking together in the same direction." So it was with us. We were separate persons who traveled in complementary rhythms on close and parallel lines.

Our intimacy widened easily and naturally until we were lovers as well as friends, yet sex never played a predominant part in our togetherness. Our main feeling was compatibility in thought and action—in trust, consideration, and respect. Fond affection meant more to us than a sex-oriented life. I loved him as a man and Scott loved me as a woman, but sex was not paramount.

Scott had lived a full and normal sexual life and had been married for years. I had no more than mildly experimented with boys' romantic attentions, and felt happily ready to live and sleep with Scott and no more than that. Perhaps the sexually unfulfilled love with Krishnamurti helped condition me for such. More than sex, I valued mutual tenderness and close contact on every level. Sex was a natural function and had its place in the full expression of the body, but was only one way, and a secondary one at that, to attaining unity with a loved one. What we had attained was a deep, emotional friendship and love, each one adjusting to the other's needs for "space in our togetherness," to use Kahlil Gibran's words.

In our early years together, when traveling, we rented separate rooms, upon mutual agreement, for the sake of independence. This resulted in hilarious situations, as in Venice, for instance, where a puzzled landlady, who had only one room to rent, said, "I can put up a curtain between the beds, if you like." In freewheeling Russia in the 1930s we were assured, "You can have a room together even though you are not married." Doing research at the Kiel Weltwirtschaft Institut in Germany we rented two desirable balconied rooms, one above the other, in a pleasant, small hostel beside the harbor. It became obvious to us that we were staying in a house of prostitution when we met new young sailors and girls in the corridors every night. There we were eminently questionable because we had *separate* rooms. What were we—spies?

In the 1920s and 1930s in America, nice girls did not live, unmarried, with men. I never considered this prohibition. We took up living together then as easily as it is done now, more than a half century later. Scott was by then separated from his wife, Nellie Seeds, though they were not divorced. Scott and I did not marry until Nellie died in 1947. By that time the alliance had been well tested and no formality was necessary to hold us together, but I wanted to share his bad name so I proposed the move. We happened to be in California at the time, Scott giving a course of lectures in Los Angeles. The minister of the Unitarian Church there tied the knot, in his secretary's apartment. He used some words from Kahlil Gibran's *The Prophet* and assured us, "No one I've ever married became divorced." We went to the town clerk's office to make it all legal. On the way Scott asked me, "Do you want a ring?" "No." "Do you want flowers?" "No."

We rarely from then on, if ever, used the words "my husband" or "my wife," as these savored too much of bondage and possession. Our living together and our eventual marriage were an alliance of two congenial souls. Broad common interests, similar curiosities, desire for simple healthful physical living conditions, all generated the love that made it a true marriage.

Felicitating me on my luck in finding Scott, a woman wrote me: "It is only in the peace movement that I sometimes run into people with a high degree of selflessness, who are always thinking of others collectively instead of their own petty, personal frustrations. But none of them equal the utter selflessness of Scott. Because of your relationship to him, you are one of the richest women that I ever met."

Agreeing with that, I made this notation for myself: "If I were fashioning a love for myself, a boon companion, I would want someone just like Scott: wise, experienced, kindly, quiet—even silent—but vocal when queried; unpretentious; handsome but not vain; competent in all things but no show-off; serious, but humorous, too; with deep emotions but restrained. . . . And if I were fashioning the ideal woman for him? Someone somewhat like me, but more serious, more articulate, more brains, more talent, more persistent, more spiritual, greater and beautiful in every way. That I would wish for him."

I must here interpolate a Sufi tale garnered from who

knows where. Nasruddin and a friend were sitting in a café drinking tea and talking about life and love. "How come you never got married, Nasruddin?" asked his friend at one point. "Well," said Nasruddin, "To tell you the truth, all my life I have looked for the perfect woman. One after another would seem just right, but there would always be something missing. Then one day, I met her. She was beautiful, intelligent, generous, kind, and we seemed to have everything in common. In fact, she was perfect." "Well, then," said his friend, "what happened? Why didn't you marry her?" Nasruddin sipped his tea reflectively. "I'll tell you," he replied. "It's a sad thing. It seems she was looking for the perfect man."

In our case, I found the perfect man for me and he was at least reconciled to the less than perfect in me.

That he appreciated me as I was shows in these two letters, received from him while he was off on lecture trips in 1932-33.

Dearest & Best:

Your two nice notes came this morning. Also the papers that you sent. Thank you so much for both. You are a darling and you so busy—to write so faithfully. Your schedule reads like the date-book of the season's most successful debutante.

You were evidently cut out to be a social being. And it seems that my influence keeps you in seclusion. Only don't run yourself ragged before the end of the month. I want at least a thread or two left when I get back to N.Y.C. . . .

You are a vigorous and well-developed person who needs room to grow in. When I am around, you do not always have room enough. These next few weeks will give you a superlative chance to do some growing. Make the most of them, for I shall be back before you know it, hemming you in once again.

Really, I shall not be away at all. Each morning and evening and many times during the day and night we shall be together. So make the next weeks a record period of growth for you and of communion and comradeship for us.

I love you, Helen. You are my dear and close friend and comrade. All good to you.

Scott

From Toledo he wrote:

I had a chance to sleep out on the porch last night. I slept very well, and was again very close to you. I bless you, sweetheart, every day. No matter where you are or what you are doing, I am with you, offering help if I can, and quite willing to stand aside if I am not needed. But always eager to share my life with you and to share yours as far as you wish to share it. My great concern is that you should always be your wholest, finest self. You are one of the very few people I know who lives on the spiritual plane. You can get there easily. It is a rare and important capacity and should be treasured and used to the utmost.

There were times, however, when he had to poke or pull me along toward his own rare intense level of dedication to the job at hand. When we were separated while I was in Europe in 1929, he wrote me, almost despairingly, a birthday letter:

When, dear friend, when, highly gifted and endowed spirit—when will you step out into the open, poised, sure, steady, determined, and make your fight and build your life? When will you leave the play-ground for the work-bench? When will you place your hand to the plow and begin turning the long furrow? The race needs grain. The field must be plowed, dragged, seeded. The harvest must be gathered. When does your day's work begin?

a. You have a fine musical talent,—that is, a talent in the field which furnishes us with what is perhaps our most perfect medium of communication.

b. You have a keen sense of beauty. You respond easily and eagerly to form, line, color, movement—to flowers, to stars.

c. You easily grasp the larger truths and relate them effectively and with understanding. You are largely free, therefore, of superstitions.

d. You have a facile and powerful personality, which attracts people, so that you may lead them or teach them, or sympathize with them and encourage them.

e. You have a capacity for organizing and directing.

How very few of us are equally gifted! This is a unique endowment. A rare being thus equipped with unusual talents, with a unique fund of power,—why should she hesitate and question and grow cold and indifferent to the throbbing possibilities of her life?

I know of one chief answer: because she has been living on the decaying social system—living upon its income, accepting, more or less, its values and standards, feeling the hopelessness and worthlessness of both values and standards; trying to forget her pain and her sense of loss by following the futile sense-satisfying practices of those who are a part of this decaying social order.

But, dear friend, this is all so transitory—so obviously passing. The beginnings of a new social order are everywhere so clearly being made. The new possibilities are so immense. The opportunities to broaden life for the mass of humanity are so great just now that there is no reason for hopelessness, no cause for cynicism, no real reason for despair.

You have your ten talents of ability. We need just those talents to make the world a better place to live in; to make the human race more understandingly capable of living in that world. What more could you—what more can anyone ask than the chance to put those immense possibilities of yours to work.

Across the distance that separates us, without separation, I greet and love the you of deep down—the you of power and understanding, the you we need so sorely, the you I have felt so often, the you I have seen so rarely. Dear Helen, some day—soon—I shall meet that you, face to face—insofar as I am worthy, and I shall strive each day to become worthy. Before that you I feel very humble and very much blessed in its presence. It is the real Helen—the Helen that I honor and respect and love.

Several long letters followed, notably this one:

Comment on your letter of August 1 re: freedom. To quote you: "I feel a free woman. Planless as a bird and happy as a bird and clean and fleet-winged as a bird. . . . I don't want to get caught in the wheel of people and society. . . . I must be free of people and things."

This is excellent up to a certain point. You are winning (have won) your freedom from the environment of Ridgewood and New York. This is a big point gained. Hold fast to it. *But free for what?* Lately you have been physically free of Ridgewood, but each day you have done something with your time. What? Have you been "free of people and things"? Impossible. You have been in daily contact with people and things. The form of this contact determines the answer to the question: "Free for what?" It determined how you have used this freedom.

If you are busy or preoccupied, please do not read further now. Lay the following pages aside until you have some leisure and can read them thoughtfully and carefully. I have written them thoughtfully. For three days I have dodged the duty of writing them. Only this morning, very early, something said to me "Get up and write that comment." It was 4:15. I was sleepy, but I got up and went to work.

I. *Theoretical Comment*
   1. Freedom is a relative term. It means, for us humans, clearing out old rubbish preparatory to a new construction. (This new construction, in its turn, must later be cleared up.)
   2. As we get free from the task or from one kind of task, we turn to another. Freedom is the transition from one life task to another. A chance to choose a new task.

3. As we grow strong enough to handle a small task, we are freed from that to take on a larger one. This is part of the essential process of growth.

4. Birds can see in two dimensions. People deal in three, four, five or more dimensions, depending on the extent of their advancement. Each new dimension leads to communications—to restrictions—to obligations. The more the dimensions, the more are those who use them responsible for their parts in the building of life. You cannot be "free as a bird". . . . You are on another plane, in another world. . . . You must be free as the freest beings on your plane of development.

II. *Certain Applications of these Theoretical Points*

1. In a world where the food and clothes you use daily are produced under the labor conditions that you sampled in NYC last spring in your factory work, you cannot be free of an obligation to help produce food and clothes.

2. In a world where oppression is rife, you cannot be free of an obligation to help root out slavery. (Debs: "While there is a lower class, I am in it; while there is a criminal element, I am of it; while there is a man in jail, I am not free.")

3. In a world of suffering, a person who could, and still can, relieve the suffering by a touch of her hand, cannot be free of the responsibility for the use of that gift or power.

4. In a world of struggle, where members of the race are agonizing over their failures, a person who can reach people and help them to get back on their feet—a person who has a genius for reaching the heart and refilling it with courage cannot be free of this vital obligation.

5. In the task of uplifting the race, those in advance cannot be free of the duty to help lift.

III. *Free for What?*

1. I asked this question at the beginning of this comment. Now I shall give what I believe to be the current answer,

though I am not in the possession of all the facts—only a tiny part of them.

2. You and I spent last winter and spring building up an energy fund and working out a plan of activity that would make it possible for you:
   a. to acquire a technique that would make you economically independent;
   b. to build a higher life through meditation, study, thought;
   c. and thus, to develop the great talents that are in keeping of You.

3. Let me put the next statement in the form of a question, because I am ill-equipped with the facts. Since I left, have you
   a. made any serious effort to gain a technique that will make you economically independent;
   b. done any consecutive, serious meditating;
   c. occupied yourself with any consecutive, serious reading or study;
   d. done any serious, consecutive, hard, quiet thinking along any line?

4. If you answer any of these questions in the affirmative, I can only say that there has been no shred of evidence to that effect in any of your letters. On the contrary, they have contained statements that you were "sky-shouting"; "racing around"; and from your last letter this gem: "I'm off for an all day sun-bath, in company with four devoted and amusing swains."
   a. They are "devoted" (and presumably take you seriously):
   b. You are "amused," "playing all day" and playing "with *them*."
   c. Wasn't it five devoted amusing swains who saw you off when you first went to Holland?

5. If my guess is correct, you have employed your freedom thus far to enable your personality (your lower self) to have its fling, and to thrust into the background those previous

qualities whose use means so much in your own development and in the service that you can render your fellows. Face this question: For the last ten weeks, what percentage of the time has been devoted to the higher and what percentage to the lower self?

6. In one of your letters you called it a "vacation." From the standpoint of your higher self, it has been a debauch. You have squandered your time and your energy on activities that mean little or nothing in terms of the higher life.

7. If my analysis is correct (and you will realize from this distance I cannot be too sure of any of these items of fact) thus far you have been using your freedom like a bird, to meet the promptings of the present and the immediate. But birds build nests and raise families and take responsibility for their well-being. Have you gone even that far? No, you have gone only to the point where you "must be free of people and things." That is irresponsible.

8. Freedom for what, beloved? Think this question over. It goes to the root of the whole structure of life. Did we both work so hard to free you from Ridgewood in order that you might turn around to walk back into Ridgewood and your old associations?

Scott continued his counsels in a September 1930 letter:

In my last letter I wrote a comment on your statements about your freedom. Here I want to add something about my idea of the opportunities and obligations that present themselves to people at our level of evolution.

I. *What I, as a member of the human race at this stage of evolution am responsible for*

1. Personal
   a. To develop, and insofar as possible, to perfect the vehicles (moral, mental, emotional, and physical) through which I work. To put the right kind of materials into them and to make them, as far as I can, structurally perfect.

b. To use these vehicles, at all times, as effectively as possible. That is, most efficiently for the advancement of the race aims.

c. To use them in that field, or in those fields, where I can do the most for race evolution.

2. Social

a. To help my fellows by trying to eliminate slavery and oppression in every form. To help make social institutions that will be as liberative as possible.

b. To help open doors of opportunity to any member of the race who is sufficiently advanced to go through the door.

c. To participate in building the very fiber of race life.

3. Cosmic

a. Being one with beauty, truth, love, which are three names for the same thing.

b. Expressing this at-oneness, working at it deliberately and consciously.

c. Drawing others into this circle: beauty—truth—love.

II. *My pack is on my back*

1. Figuratively, now; literally in a few weeks, I shall be facing the world with my pack on my back. Almost all of the other worldly possessions that I had will have been disposed of—mostly thrown away, or, where anyone else would use them, given away.

2. I want to seek, above all else, wisdom. To know how to direct feeling and thought.

3. This is a quest, in a very real and sincere sense. It is not a publicity stunt. It will not be done in the limelight. It will be done, not with the approval but against the opposition of most of my friends, who of course think that I am a little crazy. It is a search after life's real values.

4. Specifically, I hope to do the following:

a. Eliminate things, and give over every form or activity that looks toward the exercise of power. This means getting out of politics; I did it last spring.

b. Collect and organize the material necessary to work out an adequate theory and technique of world organization. A theory and practice that will make it possible for the race to function as a unit, and thus eliminate some of the conflict, such as that generated by war and class division and class war. This job has never yet been done, so far as I know.

c. Get the necessary language tools with which to do this job. At the moment this means German and Russian, because we will be travelling in those countries.

d. To live, day by day, as superbly and completely as I can, and still pursue these objectives. This means, each day: nature, bread labor, contact with people, search for truth and beauty and cosmic contacts.

III. *Can we go on at least part of this quest together?*

1. Are you not concerned, and deeply concerned, with just these things? When we have talked them over I have felt you were.

2. Is there not a field here in which we can work jointly, each following his own bent, and yet both doing many of these things?

3. Is this not the basis for our comradeship during the days and months that we have been together?

4. If this is the basis, then our comradeship should be a very real one, because this basis is a broad and solid one. On it we should be able to go far, and to good purpose.

5. Whenever I think of the work we are trying to do I become convinced that we should stick together for that. I am convinced that there is something real connected with that job—something that we can do together, and that neither of us could do as well alone.

After I had tackled a big research job he wrote me the following letter:

I think we may be able to do some really fine things together, and it makes me feel particularly happy because you seem
to want the same thing, and to feel much the same way about it.
I am particularly glad of the work you are doing now, because it
enables you to open up an intellectual field of your own. So
many women follow tamely behind their lovers—with the tail-
end of the intellectual interests the lovers happen to have. It is so
very important for you to have your independent interests in
which you are working, and also for us to have our intellectual
interests in common. This period gives you a chance to build
your own intellectual life and I am so happy that you are availing
yourself of the opportunity and doing a good job.

My dear, the thing that I am most concerned about is that
we should be able to make all of the necessary minor adjustments, and do some real pieces of work together during these
next few years. Until this winter, I was not sure whether you
would really want to do anything like that. There are so many
other things that you might want to do more than that. But I
have always felt in you that yearning for knowledge and for wisdom that must lie behind all really creative work. And I have
hoped that you might like to go in for some really serious tasks.
There are so many just now that need doing.

So you can imagine how happy I have been this winter when
you pitched into the task on your own account, and seemed to
get so much out of it. There is so much to get, dear friend, if one
only goes at it right. And I have a feeling that you know just how
to go at it. It is a part of your heritage—equipment. Just as your
feeling for music is another part.

Also it is so very important that you have gone toward the
revolutionary movement of your own volition. I could not drag
you there, and yet that is the direction in which we must both
go.

For more permanent quarters than a single room in Greenwich Village we sought and found a bare flat on the fifth floor

of a tenement building on Avenue C and Fourteenth Street, one of the poorest slum sections of downtown New York City at the time. The halls were icy in winter, the rooms also, except for heat maintained in a tiny wood stove which we stoked with coal and with wood we picked up in the street. We paid twenty dollars a month for this three-room cold-water flat, with a toilet out in the chilly hall and a tiny tub up on legs next to the kitchen sink.

Scott's lecture earnings were almost zero; he scraped a meager income from odd talks given here and there. Royalties no longer came in on the books he had written as the publishers had taken them off their lists and remaindered them. We were as poor as church mice, buying our food from the neighboring street barrows.

How did I react to this enforced poverty? For all my bourgeois background, I was willing and able to live frugally, as long as it was not ugly or sordid. The flat was bright with bargain garden furniture and sun coming in its many windows. I knew my parents disapproved strongly of my new life and Scott's influence on their beloved daughter. When Scott happened to come to the Ridgewood bungalow, my father would go out the back door. I could expect no support from them in my chosen course.

My life was taken up with typing Scott's manuscript and my research with him in the New York Public Library. He had just finished his first and only novel, *Free Born*, and was trying to market it. It was the story of a young black boy who, though born free in the South, had led a persecuted and disadvantaged life. His education and emergence from oppression were taken from real life people Scott had met while researching for his book on the Negro situation, *Black America*. The book ended with the young man jailed for political activity. Scott could not find a publisher who would handle the explosive material, so he finally had to get it out himself in 1932.

Life may have been bare and frugal for us, but it was contented and productive.

We Take to the Woods
of Vermont

When the sun rises, I go to work;
When the sun goes down, I take my rest;
I dig the well from which I drink,
I farm the soil that yields my food.
I share the creation, Kings can do no more.

Chinese, 2500 B.C.

*I*T WAS SCOTT who first broached the possibility of our leaving the city and going to live in the country, where we could at least grow our own food. He did not want or intend to flee his social obligations, but we had to earn our living somehow and it was increasingly difficult to get along in the city on our slim budget.

In the fall of 1932 he took a trip to a wilderness section of southern Vermont to look for suitable land at a possible price. It was during the Great Depression when real estate was cheap. He returned with a purchase plan in his pocket. He had found an old wooden house on sixty-five acres of poor land on a dirt road in the mountains. We could have it for three hundred dollars down and an eight-hundred-dollar mortgage. This we could manage. On a cold cheerless day in November, we packed our few New York belongings and migrated to our new life.

A somewhat similar situation was described in a 1911 book called *A Few Acres and a Cottage*, by F. E. Green: "There was no going back now. I had thrown up my post and was rapidly sinking my little capital on the great venture in the open country. By some means I should have to wrest a living from the soil. There was no nest-egg to fall back on, no private income to butter my bread. I had gotten down to the bed-rock of existence. Now I should feel something of the exhilaration of contending with Nature, winning bread from the bare earth, and know the joy of creating something with my own hands and completing that which I had fashioned. It is in the lack of creative joy that is to be found the insidious germ of that soul-deadening, manhood-destroying effect of city life, where the worker is only an unrecognized cog in a huge industrial machine."

To live in the country was something new for me. Summer vacations on lordly estates or at summer camps beside lakes were more my custom, but I adapted well to the enforced frugal life. I found it wonderfully satisfying to be in close contact with nature every day, to feel the earth under my feet, to be away from noise and clamor. I learned to live in simple conditions of housing, on simple local food, to wear old clothing, and to get rid of unnecessary belongings.

I adapted surprisingly well to Vermont backwoods conditions. I even came to relish privations. I preferred our sparsely furnished, gaunt, uninsulated farmhouse to the comfortable, cluttered and carpeted, overheated suburban homes I had known. I enjoyed the sparse fare we lived on. Something in me likes to be cold when other people are toasting round a fire; to fast when others are feasting; to work when others are lounging. As with Scott, there is something of an ascetic and puritan in me.

We had several ideals in mind. The Tao Te Ching advised:

In dwelling be close to the land.
In meditation, go deep into the heart.
In dealing with others, be gentle and kind.
In speech, be true.
In ruling, be just.
In business, be competent.
In action, watch the timing.

Scott began to teach me practical skills: work with tools, shovels, axe, and saw; gardening; forestry; building construction; masonry—all of which he had learned on his grandfather's farm in rural Pennsylvania. What Aldous Huxley said of D. H. Lawrence could similarly be said of Scott: "He regarded no task as too humble for him to undertake, nor so trivial that it was not worth his while to do it well. He could cook and he could sew; he could darn a stocking and milk a cow; he was an efficient wood-cutter. . . . Fires always burned which he had kindled."

I learned to build and tend the wood fires that heated the house with wood we cut ourselves. I learned to cook, to make soups, to bake potatoes, to cut up farm apples for applesauce. There was plenty of indoor and outdoor work to occupy us in the first winter. And when spring came we planted a large garden and started to live off the land.

Gardening was our first outdoor work together. We dug and cultivated a garden space in the likeliest place near the house. I learned to plant and harvest, and to weed. This latter became a special sport and never a chore. It was a delight to me to leave clean rows behind. Providing one's own food from one's own garden became wonderfully satisfying. I was learning the gratification of gardening, which Scott had learned years before and practiced in the Arden community in Delaware. I observed his skills and learned from them but never felt subservient. He was never the boss nor I the underling. He treated me as an equal, never dominating, though I was a novice, never having handled tools before in my life. My hands had been kept clean for the violin. I had hardly swept a floor or boiled an egg or picked a berry before. There was much to learn and enjoy and I took to it with a will.

Scott wrote to me early in our stay, when he was away lecturing: "You dug 58 ridges in the garden? What a splendid job for those few days! Doesn't it give you a thrill to feel that it is well done? It came to me that now for the first time you probably know what a keen joy there is in just digging the earth. It is wonderful if you have learned that lesson. Many folk go through life and never find it out."

Emerson wrote in 1870: "He who digs a well, constructs a stone fountain, plants a grove of trees by the roadside, plants an orchard, builds a durable house, reclaims a swamp or so much as puts a stone seat by the wayside, makes the land so far lovely and desirable, makes a fortune which he cannot carry away with him, but which is useful to his country long afterwards."

We worked in the woods together, clearing spaces between the trees, cutting down the spindly and dead ones and thus getting our winter fuel. I learned the differences between oak and maple and ash and elm and the properties of each. And sometimes, a miss-hit with the axe or hatchet would send me running for home and bandages. I never became as adept as Scott, who was a master woodsman.

We wanted to try natural organic farming with no chemical fertilizers; few if any mechanical tools, therefore a minor amount of technology; a natural diet, locally grown and simple, as unprocessed as possible, mostly raw and uncontaminated. We sought natural living in simple wholesome surroundings.

We aimed at a use economy as far from the money system as possible, but we needed some cash to buy gas for our truck, to pay local taxes, and to get several food incidentals. We considered selling firewood and lumber from our woodlot but everyone roundabout had plenty of their own. In the next year a former Dutch suitor of mine died and left me a small legacy. With it we bought the farm next door which had a fine stand of maple trees on it.

Soon thereafter, in September 1934, Scott wrote: "After next year I should like us to treat the Vermont enterprise as a financially self-sustaining unit. We don't care to make anything out of it in the way of money, but I think it should carry itself and feed us while we are there. With care and management this should be easy, once we get the sugar bush going. That alone, in good years, should pay all the taxes and insurance, and in a few years it should pay for the investment in sugar tools and for the development of the sugar bush."

Scott organized the clearing of the maple grove, leaving only the best trees; he devised and laid out a grid of seven miles of galvanized pipe up into the woods which would carry sap down to the sugar house. I helped tap out and gather the maple sap, and then went down to the sugarhouse and boiled long hours to make the hundreds of gallons of syrup a year that eventually earned us a fair living.

We sold the syrup at the farm or through mail orders. Part of the crop we put through a further process. Over the kitchen stove at home we boiled the syrup until it crystallized. We then poured the soft sugar into pound tins, forming "gold bricks," or into rubber molds in the shapes of stars, trees, daisies, or rabbits, boxing them as "Picture Packs" and selling them by the dozens in shops and roadside stands.

In after-years Scott wrote: "I was thinking what success you have had in developing techniques of making, packaging and selling syrup and sugar. You could have built up an impressive business!" But this we did not do. When we had as many orders for our products as we needed, we stopped work at it and took a trip or started a new book.

Whenever I was near a good library I would frequent the rare-book rooms and look up what I could find on the origins of the tapping of maples and sugar making. I showed the research to Scott and he opined: "With all that historic material, and our apprenticeship in learning the sugar business, our failures and successes in the bush, you have a book there."

We worked at it together, and it became *The Maple Sugar Book* which is still, nearly forty years later, the classic volume on the subject, full of historic references and quotations on ancient procedures, plus our own experiences learning the ropes. A publisher was easily found in Pearl Buck and her husband Richard Walsh, of the John Day Company, who came up to Vermont from New York with the manuscript to consult and to see us. Pearl was so excited with what we were doing with our lives in the wild woods that she suggested we tackle another book, dealing more generally with our whole enterprise: our organic gardening and forestry practices, our whole-food vegetarianism, our building methods, our relations with neighbors in the valley. All of this would later be incorporated into our book, *Living the Good Life*.

Living the good life for us was practicing harmony with the earth and all that lives on it. It was frugal living, self-subsistent, self-sustaining. It was earning our way by the sweat of our brows, beholden to no employer or job. It was growing our own food, building our own buildings, cutting our own wood, and providing for our own livelihood. We needed and used little money. If we couldn't pay for a thing, we made it ourselves or did without.

Our idea was to take care of our physical needs, housing, food, fuel, and clothing so that we could read, write, study, teach, or make music without dependence on the outside world, and to do this together. "If we had ample means and could choose any kind of life we wished," wrote Gove Hambidge in his 1935 book *Enchanted Acre: Adventures in Backyard Farming*, "we would choose what we have chosen. And when I say we, I mean we. There are many differences between a man's viewpoint and a woman's in the same house, year in and year out. But there must be a profound unshaken unity underneath the differences if they are to make a success of such a life as we have lived, because the things that must be passed by are things that one or the other might consider indispensible."

Scott and I attained that unity and lived in tune with each other.

As to any regrets Scott might have had on the secluded life he was living in the country with me, he felt he had done what he could in public—not with great success or recognition, but the best he could. Now that phase was over, so far as he knew, and he took great pleasure in his contacts with nature and real delight in being able to improve the soil and environment. I sensed no resentment or bitterness in him at being shunted off into oblivion, with only occasional public lecturing or publishing possibilities. One friend commented: "Too bad; he has burned all his bridges." But Scott was building new bridges.

It seemed possible, even likely, that fate had more in store for him than a mere professorship in a major university. His influence was to grow to include more than classes in schoolrooms. His range broadened until he was learning and teaching in a larger school than ever. Even in the beginning of our Vermont sojourn, stray visitors dropped in to see what we were up to, and later they crowded in. In carrying out our own particular life style, Scott and I were embarked on a novel and worthwhile adventure which was apparently to serve as a guidepost to other venturers into self-subsistent homesteading.

We saw our good life not as a model for others but as a pilgrimage, for us, to the best way we could conceive of living. We felt a glad responsibility in joining with the stream of onward life, with the whole magnificent enterprise. This was living a life of affirmation, of contribution, of making every act and every day purposeful. To live the good life, we found, was to do the best we were capable of in any set of circumstances.

With enough food and fuel to keep us going, we turned our attention to building. The old house and barn we had acquired and were living in were dilapidated and deteriorating. Should we repair the dwelling and outbuildings? We tried our hand at an addition to the house: a stone living room, building our first fireplace. This got us started and interested in further construction. There followed a log cabin, a new sugarhouse, and a three-room cottage built entirely of stone, with paneled walls and wide windows facing Pinnacle Mountain. The cabin and cottage were sold to friends at cost and we counted it all as good learning experience. In the deep woods we erected a stone cabin for Scott as a study. Still we had not moved from the first old wooden house.

Finally we felt we were ready to proceed on to a permanent stone home of our own. A huge, perfectly perpendicular rock wall in the woods inspired us for a site. It became the back wall of the living room. Against the nine-by-twenty-foot boulder we attached our four-room, two-storied house, with woodshed and sugar-packing room. I designed the format and made simple amateur drawings; there were no blueprints. The house, a Swiss-type chalet form, was drawn in a childish picture. From that we worked.

The seven-foot dip in the ground level made the house delightfully irregular, with steps up and down in every room, which was not in my original plan. I handled most of the stone while Scott and two local helpers mixed the concrete, made the window and door frames, hewed the stalwart beams, and roofed the building.

The interior was Spartan and spare. Stone floors of smooth granite from the farm gave it the appearance of a monastery. The furniture was all handmade, mainly by us. The walls were pine-paneled with broad twenty-inch locally sawed boards stained a warm brown. As in a barn, if dust gathered on the floor, it could be cleaned once a week. If cobwebs hung from the ceiling, no one noticed. It was a house au naturel, heated by fireplaces, with a wood stove in the kitchen for cooking.

We also put up a stone garage and woodshed, a stone guesthouse, toolshed, and greenhouse, more than half a dozen buildings in all. It was a monument to our industry and we thought we were settled for what was left of our lives, Scott being sixty and I, forty.

All this time Scott, when not working on the farm, was putting in time writing on economics and foreign affairs. He issued monthly a news commentary entitled *World Events*, a small one-man publication with no organizational backing, no "angel," no hat-passing, and no advertising. "No sponsorship and no censorship" was the watchword of this unique independent publication, a strictly nonprofit affair. Neither the author nor the small committee of friends in charge of printing and distribution accepted any pay for their work. This project continued for more than a dozen years, when it was merged as a World Events column with *Monthly Review*, an independent socialist magazine for which Scott wrote two hundred columns, continuing until he was close to ninety years old.

He also wrote during his time in Vermont various "Social Science Handbooks": *United World*, *The Soviet Union as World Power*, *Democracy Is Not Enough*, *The Tragedy of Empire*, *War or Peace?*, and *The Revolution of Our Time*. These were all put out

in the years 1945 to 1947 by a private press, and never adver-
tised or reviewed. Most of the scanty sales were made at Scott's
lectures.

As a true economist, Scott had strong habits of frugality and
economy: "Live within your income; spend less than you get;
pay as you go," were axioms often on his lips. He could not and
would not waste money needlessly, especially upon himself. He
preached and practiced practical economy.

Here is a report of his schedule, living quarters, and diet
while on a lecture trip in the United States in the 1940s:

> The first day in Madison I spoke three times; today, four, all
> to small groups. I will probably get my carfare out of it. I took a
> hotel room; people keep you up so late in private homes. When
> you get back from a meeting: 'Sorry I couldn't go. Now tell me
> *all* you said.' And the business begins all over again. This room is
> satisfactory and costs $1.25 per day. It's a small hotel beside the
> railroad station; a bit noisy but otherwise alright.

From Detroit he wrote:

> Have been here just one week (paid $7) and have worked out
> an excellent routine—breakfast: oranges and a few dates; lunch: 1
> or 1 1/2 heads of lettuce and 1/2 pint sour cream and a little
> honey; evening: tomato juice after the lecture. Also at some time
> during the day, usually a small can of some juice—carrot, grape-
> fruit, apple, etc. I have kept exceptionally well on this diet. Feel
> fine and do not tire. Since coming to Detroit I have not eaten an
> egg or taken a grain of starch—except in dates. Have bought two
> avocados at 10 cents each. I think of you when I eat them. Each
> night but one I have walked to the meetings. Takes me from 6:50
> to 8:05, about 4 1/2 to 5 miles.

This was all in line with his "have less, be more" philosophy. One time at a clothing sale I found for him a particularly

fine overcoat (he needed one) reduced from one hundred dollars to fifty dollars. It was warm, of the best material and cut, and was just his size. He would not let me buy it as he did not want to wear an expensive coat at *any* price.

Witness a letter he wrote to a friend, a topflight tailor in Carmel, California, who had made him a suit for a present:

> The last mail brought the beautifully made suit which you say you made for me. It was very fine, indeed, of you to make the suit and I do appreciate it. Such acts of friendship are comparatively rare and all the more welcome.
>
> At the same time, you must remember that I am a workingman. Beside my work clothes, I have only one suit—never more. That suit is made of serviceable Scottish tweed, warm enough for New England winters. I scarcely ever wear it from Easter to early November, when I need it for lecturing. Usually it lasts three to four years. When it is worn out I get another. I never have dressy or sporty clothes of any kind. I wear sweaters.
>
> This is a policy based on choice, not necessity. I was brought up in a family that was always well off and I have never lacked money enough to dress well. But, I do not believe one man should have an abundance of what others might lack, and I do not believe in fashion or style. I do not believe in pampering habits of the body and mind that give a feeling of superiority that the well-dressed people almost always possess. Such a point of view is bad for tailoring, but is, I believe, socially sound.
>
> Incidentally, I carry the theory to one pair of shoes, one hat (worn only in cold weather), one overcoat, a tie or two, a belt and that is all.
>
> Excuse this case history, but I wanted to give you an idea what sort of person I am: trying to live by ascetic, idealistic principles, rather than according to opportunist choices. It in no way diminishes my appreciation of your kindness.

I might add here my own story of economy in the matter of clothing. Scott and I were on a platform together speaking on the simple life. At question time a man got up in the audience and said: "I own a clothing store in town. You've been talking about simplicity. I know my values. That suit you are wearing, Mrs. Nearing, I judge to cost one-hundred-fifty dollars at least." This remark caused a gasp from the audience. My answer was glad and instant. "I'm happy you told me that. I got it the other day in a thrift shop for five dollars." The audience roared.

My mother had been a habitual shopper and often trailed me behind her through the endless aisles of Macy's huge department store in New York City. I absorbed some of her needlessly extravagant buying ways. I might go into Macy's for a pair of stockings and come out also with a bargain sweater, a scarf, or a book. But I also had a very thrifty side, saving blank sides of paper from the vast tide of inflowing printed matter, and recycling envelopes from incoming mail. I made great balls of string from opened packages and tucked them away for future use.

Scott applied to me a story he had heard of a little old lady in a poor section of New York City who was a congenital hoarder. After her death, searchers ransacking the tiny flat found paper bags full of string and labeled "Might Come In Useful." One box was found with the notation "String Too Small To Save."

He also recounted the story of a woman who was so economical that she couldn't bear to throw away partly used bottles from the medicine cabinet. I had that propensity, too, perhaps a dangerous one. She downed them all during intervals of time. The most difficult dose to take, she said, was the horse medicine. That far I did not go!

One hot summer month, Scott was asked to speak at a peace conference in Colombo, Sri Lanka. He had only his one good suit, the winter one. I was concerned as to what he could wear and how much a new suit for the occasion would cost. I happened to be in a secondhand store, looking for clothes to send to friends in Poland who needed warm winter things, when I saw a fine gray flannel suit that looked Scott's size. I went to the library where he was writing. "Would you wear a secondhand suit?" I asked him. "Why not?" he replied. Over to the store we went and he tried on the suit. It fit at the shoulders, the waist, the cuffs and was the right length. Paying less than fifteen dollars for it, he had a ready-made suit for the conference.

A good part of our clothing came from such sources. Scott could go into a large department store for a pair of shoelaces and come out with only those, shaking his head about the amount of things he had seen and did not need. It is told that Socrates, looking around the market where all an Athenian wanted lay piled in glowing confusion, exclaimed: "Bless me, what a lot of things there are a man can do without."

Scott sought a higher standard of life rather than a higher standard of living. "It's what you are, not what you have on that is important in life," Scott has said. "I regard being and doing as the essential ingredients of life; merely living and having can be an obstruction and burden. It's not what we have but what we do with what we have that constitutes the real value of life. . . . "

At banquets or dinners where he was to speak he often refused an elaborate meal, pulling out an apple or orange from his pocket and dining on that. Once at a publisher's ornate office building Scott was escorted to the service elevator and arrived by the office's rear door. "How come?" asked his astonished associates. "I guess they thought I was the plumber," chuckled Scott.

I have sat in an audience attending one or another of Scott's talks and heard women in front of me say, "He dresses like a farmer. That's the suit he wore last year." I wanted to tap them on the shoulder and say, "He *is* a farmer, and that's his one suit." He dressed decently and was always meticulously clean and neat, but he did not dress for style or fashion. He didn't want to identify himself at all with the upper classes.

As with mere possessions, Scott had little regard for money. He wrote me from Chicago in 1945: "I spoke at the Painters' Union last night. It was a very good meeting. Heretofore they have paid me $10. Last night they handed me $20, remarking, 'So as to get you up nearer to a painter's wage.'" One chairman of a meeting wrote him years later: "I recall asking you to come to Wilmington to speak for the Young Men's Hebrew Association and you said you would be glad to come. When I asked the amount of your fee you answered, 'As much as any other lecturer.' I said we paid nothing, and you replied, 'That will be my fee.'"

His disregard of self led to an odd situation at the entrance to a meeting in Coney Island at which he was to speak. An officious ticket taker who did not recognize him would not let us in without our paying. Scott paid for us both, preferring not to beat his breast and make a scene. At a large debate with Congressman Hamilton Fish in New York City, Scott could not get through the huge crowd outside. Rather than push his way through, stating that he was one of the speakers, he got behind the phalanx of guards around Mr. Fish and squeezed his way in behind them.

Scott in his time had spoken to thousands of people in great halls such as Madison Square Garden and Mecca Temple in New York, and summers at Chautauqua conventions, getting up to a thousand dollars a talk. He also spoke as willingly in small rooms at New York's Labor Temple, for instance, where thirty to fifty people attended and paid twenty-five cents admission. "Large fee or small fee," he wrote me on one of his trips, "I do not like the plan of talking for money. I would much prefer not to. If I must, I prefer to do it on what I regard as a decent basis."

We tried to keep a money relationship with the neighbors to a minimum. We occasionally hired their help in the woods and in house building and sometimes exchanged labor. Aside from these contacts we were tolerated as odd folk "from away," as they said, or outsiders, who worked as hard as they did or even harder.

Our main differences from the natives were our work habits and our diet. I have overheard remarks like: "I couldn't live without any meat." "They got no animals. No radio neither. Music though; they got music." "They eat with chopsticks, out of wooden bowls." "How'd they ever get those rocks so smooth? Chiseled 'em, I guess."

Even our growing of flowers to give away was considered strange. A friend from the city who visited us wrote the following satiric verse on "The Flower People":

> Their chief delight was growing, picking, giving away
>   sweet peas.
> When taking a trip to town in blooming season
> They filled baskets, basins, pails—with dozens of
>   bunches,
> And gave them out during the day—to friends,
>   grocers, dentist, gas station attendants,
> And utter strangers on the street.
> All were delighted recipients of the fragrant blossoms.
> I've lived too near New York too long
> To understand such practices.

I was asked occasionally to play my violin at local affairs and always obliged, though there was not much time in my busy farm life for keeping up to concert pitch. One spring day while we were hard at tapping in the sugar bush, a delegation came from nearby Londonderry, Vermont, to ask if I would play at an old lady's funeral in Bondville. The woman had said before she died, "I don't want any darned preacher preaching over me, I want Scott Nearing." So, laying down our tools, over the hill we went and helped at the funeral. I played Thais' "Meditation" and Scott spoke eloquently for the old lady we had never met. After the service some people came up and asked Scott if he did this professionally and if others could avail themselves of his services. One man was heard to say in a loud voice: "When I die, I want Helen to play at my funeral and I want Scott to speak."

Our eschewing of modern-day pleasures like the radio was considered eccentric. Scott never did learn to tolerate the intrusion of the radio into his life. He not only looked on it as trivial, trashy, and inconsequential, with news at best only in headlines, but there was no escape from its noise, which sounds now in corridors, in elevators, in shops, in banks, in airports, and in most homes.

The young Nearing and Knothe families had grown up in a comparatively noiseless era, with few motorcars, little traffic and no din, and no radio with its constant background of music or talk. We were lucky to have been from before the Age of Noise. Evenings were quiet, daytimes, too. No morning news trumpeted; one waited for the daily paper or weekly or monthly magazine to read in peace.

Quietude was close to Thoreau. The incessant rowdy radios would have maddened him and driven him from society altogether. Imagine him with a boom box or walkie-talkie in the woods. He would undoubtedly have preferred deafness to the sea of sound that hourly surrounds most of our present-day population. We are assaulted continuously. Hell, for us (and likely Thoreau), would be a place where one could not escape the bombardment of continual noise.

The television, to Scott and me, was an equal abomination, an insidious lure to waste the time of the population, especially of the children. He considered it one of the horrors of civilization. Direct experience is what we need; that's what we're here to get: experiential education, *not* through television, where we're physically separated from *doing*. It separates the individual from reality; encourages passivity; implants deleterious images directly into the unconscious; dulls awareness; gives the illusion of experience; has a hypnotic addictive quality which is totally dangerous and obnoxious. "The dreadful voices and the dressed-up artificial people one invites into one's own home through the medium!" Scott has exclaimed. "TV is slop served by second-rate minds. I'd rather chew hardtack from first-rate minds."

The telephone he called "a real intrusion; an impertinence—summoning one like a servant to any casual call." He could sit in a hotel room busily writing; the phone would ring and ring. He paid absolutely no attention but went on with his writing. During Scott's last few months I had a telephone installed, in case of emergency, yet I put it in the barn so I could use it if necessary but there would be no ringing in the house.

This had certain disadvantages. Visitors (and there were many) turned up continually without prearrangement. We never knew when strange faces would peer around the corner and we would be engulfed by pilgrims.

Evenings we were usually alone. Without either television or radio to clutter up our evenings we settled around the fire with fine old classics, as the Brontë family might have done. One or the other of us read aloud as beans or peas were shelled, soup or applesauce made, or knitting or darning was done— Scott doing as many of these homely tasks as I did. Tolstoy, Victor Hugo, Emerson, Thoreau, Shakespeare, the poets—all were read and reread.

We also shared contemporary books and articles that had turned up in our daytime reading or newspapers and books in which we were doing research. My favorite books to read out loud were Olive Schreiner's, Dunsany's, and Blackwood's fantasy tales, accounts of UFOs, and books about animals. We planned to do another book (and I may get to it later) to be called "Telling Tales" or "Tales To Be Told," a collection of the fables, stories, and poems which enthralled us and which we read together again and again. Many were definitely fanciful and esoteric, picked out by me, including science fiction as well and, if Scott chose, stories of social significance. All were enjoyed by both of us.

I had a consuming curiosity as to the authorship of Shakespeare's plays and poems and collected around forty books on this debated topic. I could not believe the unlearned, uneducated Stratford man had composed them. He left only three wobbly "Shagsper" signatures, not a book in his library, not a page of manuscript; his daughters were illiterate. Was he, too? I would have liked to join Emerson's proposed club of readers who questioned the authorship of Shakespeare's sonnets. In one of his *Journals* he brought up the controversial questions: "Who is the author? To whom were they written? What do they mean?" This tickled me and was right up my alley. Scott called it my "detective story mania."

One day a week, usually Sunday, we gave our digestive system (and whoever cooked) a rest, by eliminating our already light breakfast and lunch and fasting during the day. Having no scheduled activity except perhaps a walk or a swim, or putting up a bit of stone wall, we took the day easy. These fasting days were ended in the evening by the fire with a supper of popcorn, carrot juice or cider, and selections from my four hundred or more classical phonograph records played late into the night.

We also fasted for ten days at a time at least once a year as a sort of vacation from food. We drank only water for that time and lessened our work schedule. We looked forward to periods of abstinence and believed we benefited in body and mind, and gained extra time for reading and writing.

In wintertime, when farm activity was slight, Scott would accept requests to lecture in various parts of the country, leaving me happily alone at home with my reading, writing, and music. I tended the mail, filled orders for books, sent packages of books to him to be sold at his meetings, and generally kept the farm going. I enjoyed traveling with him, when I did it, and treasured the time alone without him, getting some writing of my own done. A large part of *The Maple Sugar Book* was a project of one of my Vermont winters alone, in 1948.

Scott always left our country home reluctantly, and yet he accepted invitations to speak whenever he felt he had something to contribute. In the 1940s he wrote to me: "It was a difficult adjustment from Vermont to the lecture platform and the trains. Vermont seems so logical and sensible, and this seems so artificial and forced! After a couple of weeks I do not mind it so much, but at the outset it seems very tough indeed."

In an undated letter of the same period he wrote:

> I am still in a daze. I cannot get accustomed to the noise, confusion and turmoil. It is really dreadful. I feel as though I never want to leave Vermont again. Usually when I start on this grind, I strike a day when I just feel that I cannot go on with it. How I wished, these last four days, that I was up in the quiet hills! Every year I say that never again will I try seven days a week of talks. Yet I have had seven days beginning November 28 and it will go on till December 23. I should really stick to the six day or even five day schedule another year. I seem to live but do not learn.

He wrote me a poignant letter from Chicago, December 13, 1948.

> Williams and I did not settle up for Saturday's meeting, so I went there tonight to see him. He made a gamble. Took a larger hall and put a $12 ad in the paper. He took in $47 all told. Hall and ad cost him $22. Balance $25. This represented (1) my travelling expenses and (2) the very considerable amount of work he had put in on the meeting, plus (3) my talking for four hours.
>
> It costs me more than $20 per day to pay carfare and board-and-keep on these long jumps. But I took $20 and left the $5 for him. This meant that I got nothing for talking and nothing for the long hard push up here from D.C. and then going from train to meeting hall and talking all evening.
>
> I have been watching things closely this winter. Roxanna [his booking agent] had got me one date for which she gave me $70. To keep this date cost me at least $30. That will be my one really commercial date this winter. The Friends Service Committee dates in Ohio and the Community Churches in Boston and New York are semi-commercial. If I added up all of them together, I would not be getting enough to pay my room rent on the N.Y.C. downtown east-side—let alone buy food and clothing. It is truly staggering to watch these historical forces sweep over us.
>
> I walked to Williams's place and back 1 1/2 miles each way, through some of the filthiest streets and past some of the vilest taverns and dens I have seen outside the Orient. On the way back I stopped to get some tomato juice in a food shop and to get my shoes shined in a shine parlor. In the former I got a long dose of Superman in pursuit of a criminal. In the latter I heard Lowell Thomas passing out the news. I did this between 5 and 6 P.M. Christmas gaudy decorations in the streets, hurrying, harried crowds. The thing is incredible! It was a super-nightmare. I have been away from Pikes Falls for 6 weeks and travelling most of the time, but I could not believe my senses.
>
> East Coast towns were founded and built by Europeans. There is some saving sense of order and even dignity about them.

This place was built by Americans. Its only redeeming feature is the pathetic and terrifying caricatures of humanity who inhabit it. I have been in Chicago many times before. Never just at Christmas, with the contrasts and implications. I am thankful that you are in Vermont.

Tonight I know, for sure, that if we did not have the farm I would have to choose between (1) getting an old man's job, which would barely pay expenses; (2) living on an old age pension, which pays less, or (3) living on my relatives or friends and always feeling unwanted or semi-wanted. By comparison, the farm is paradise. And you can see that I fully and thankfully realize what a treasure I have in you.

This coincides exactly with Elbert Hubbard's opinion in his 1908 book *Health and Wealth*, where he says: "There are three habits which, with but one condition added, will give you everything in the world worth having, and beyond which the imagination of man cannot conjure forth a single addition or improvement. These habits are: the work habit, the health habit, the study habit. If you are a man and have these habits, and also have the love of a woman who has those same habits, you are in paradise now and here, and so is she."

Moving on to Maine

> *To withdraw gracefully from the public stage and by securing a season of virtuous repose after a life of action—to place a kind of sacred interval between this world and the next, is a piece of practical wisdom which I fear is in few hands.*
>
> Ely Bates, *Rural Philosophy*, 1907

*W*E HAD GONE to the country in 1932 not to escape from the world or from social concerns. It was the only way out for us; we had to solve the problem of livelihood. We had wanted to find a decent manner of living in order to participate and play a worthy part.

Simple frugal living we had achieved, but by the early 1950s the isolated valley we had come to was turning rapidly worldly. Former neighbors were selling out to newcomers who used their places as vacation houses and second homes. Beer parties were being held by the young people coming in. The tempo and tone of the inhabitants was changing. Old ways of living were going down the drain. Sophisticated city skiers were drifting in with fancy cars and high living. Electricity came into the valley, telephones, radio, and TV. Too many tourists and visitors were breaking in upon our solid work habits.

The disease of development helped push us from Vermont. We felt more and more uncomfortable and invaded. Could we, should we, leave our home of nineteen years and try to find another place and refuge? Could we leave our stone buildings, our thriving gardens, our maple sugar business? We were no longer as young as two decades before. We would have to find a new source of income. Did we have the courage to embark on another venture somewhere else?

There is a commitment to a loved place; there is also a beginning and an end for being somewhere. Scott was all for leaving everything behind, giving the place to someone and walking down the road with satchel in hand. I was ready to go, but it was harder for me to leave all behind than it was for him. As a woman I tended to cling at least to some possessions and to known surroundings.

I had designed the stone house we lived in. The low-roofed, balconied chalet reminiscent of my days in the Austrian Tirol and Swiss Alps was an expressive part of my being. It was my second skin. I knew by name the stones that I had put in the walls. The house was on a magnificent site at a high elevation amid rolling hills, with massive Stratton Mountain just opposite. There was a high point on the property which we called Sunset Hill where I had often climbed and meditated alone, and together with Scott. I had contacted a veritable presence there in close communion and was sad to leave it.

I had matured in Vermont from an inexperienced, naive, dependent girl into a tough and sturdy homesteader with many trades at my fingertips. All those transforming influences I would leave behind—and possibly never experience again—for life in a new state, Maine, in a wooden shack of someone else's construction, on flat land at sea level. Ah, well, I thought: Onward, ever onward. "Siempre mejor!"—always better—was an exclamation Scott often used.

We had pondered the possibilities before choosing Maine. Should we go to Europe and lodge in some tiny village in the mountains, or find a house on the dunes in Holland? We would be too widely separated from our homeland and social and political interests. Should we look for another more isolated spot in Vermont? No, we were ready for something new. Two decades in the mountains, why not try the next two decades near water, why not by the sea? Maine seemed the place to look.

I am a water witch, a dowser, and had located water on our land in Vermont. In a book on radiesthesia I had read an account of finding water by dowsing with a pendulum over a map. Why couldn't I try to find just the place we wanted with a pendulum over a map? I got a large, detailed chart of Maine and concentrated on isolated acreage, by the water, a working farm, not just a summer place. The pendulum circled over a section of upper Penobscot Bay, where the river opened out into the ocean. We got into our pickup truck and drove up the coast of Maine looking for our new home.

Nothing was possible or appealing until we came to the little hamlet of Harborside on Cape Rosier about two-thirds of the way up the Maine coast toward Canada. There on an isolated cove was an unpretentious wooden house which we could afford, on meadows overlooking Penobscot Bay, with about 140 acres. We put money down on the place and went back to Vermont to find new owners for our old Forest Farm. This was easy, as we were letting it go for half what we had put into it. Scott wanted no profit, only someone who would live there as we had, who would continue to benefit the soil and the community.

That did not happen. We sold the place to an apparently likely couple who later became real-estate developers, benefiting from the proximity of Stratton Mountain, the largest ski area in the East at the time. Our forest farm and sugar bush became cluttered with cottages and seasonal folk. Our experience was typical for rural Vermont in the past four decades.

Land prices had been very low when we came to that Vermont valley. On account of the Korean War, values had increased greatly by the time we decided to leave. Scott wanted no part of war profits, so gave his section of the acreage to the town of Winhall for a municipal forest. The town grudgingly accepted it, judging it was some sort of tax dodge. They could not conceive it was given out of the goodness of his heart. My half of the property, when sold, enabled me to buy the place in Maine.

A friend wrote me at the time, "You could have sold at a great profit. Scott gave a whole mountain away with land that became extremely valuable. You once turned down a terrific order from Macy's in New York. [This was when Macy's wanted large amounts of maple sugar candy.] You and Scott seem to go out of your way not to make money."

Scott sent me a note as we were preparing in the fall of 1951 to leave Vermont:

> You thought you might have some trouble in detaching from the Vermont house. You said that the step to Maine would be a bit of a plunge. I expected you'd feel that way. It is for that reason that the progress of activities in Maine should be well worked out, inclusive and satisfying to you. I propose that we divide up the days, spending time in the garden, getting firewood, writing, music, reading and see whether we cannot have the same sense of accomplishment that we had in Vermont.
>
> We have done a nice job there. We can be proud of it. But having done the job, if we still have time, energy and creativity, why not move on and do another nice job? We've painted that picture. Why not try another? We have made our point: homesteading can succeed and bring real satisfaction. It is not a cure-all for everybody, but it is a way of life for some. Certainly for us. Let's start again.

In the spring of 1952 we sugared for the last time (I boiled a thousand gallons) and drove out the driveway with some regret at leaving our nine stone buildings and fine gardens, but with keen anticipation of a new start. The new Forest Farm would be a challenge, yet life would be more leisurely than in Vermont, without the push of the maple sugar business.

Scott surveyed the ways of living in Maine—what cash crop would be most feasible—and settled on blueberries as indigenous and natural to the climate and soil. He picked out the best location on the farm and put in a hundred plants of hybrid varieties. From these in years to come we harvested thousands of quarts which, while not as lucrative as maple syrup or sugar, paid our running expenses and afforded us more time for other pursuits.

Again we cleared the land, cultivated and planted crops, and produced food from our gardens. We worked together daily and were satisfied we had made the right decision to leave the burgeoning ski developments for this quiet dead end in Maine.

Our lives perhaps were more social in Maine than in Vermont. Scott kept at his writing and outdoor work at his usual pace, while I had more free time to see neighbors and take care of the daily flood of visitors who, in time, dropped in on us. These chance visitors came from all over the country as well as locally. They had read one or another of our books (the first edition of *Living the Good Life* came out in 1954), had heard Scott speak, were interested in organic gardening, or were merely curious to see the place. I welcomed them, passed some on to Scott, and then usually fed one and all. One year, by body count, twenty-three hundred people—friends and strangers—knocked on our door. All seemed to profit by the experience so we continued to keep "open house."

Evidently there was a lure and attachment to this odd old couple who had stuck so determinedly to their self-imposed retreat from civilization. The visitors journeyed miles, even from India, Japan, and many European countries, to see if it was real and to witness the Good Life in action. When they came up the lane by foot or bicycle or car, rounded the bend and saw the stone constructions and flowers and neat rows of vegetables and garden, it seemed a dream come true. They left in happy hopes that they could go home and do likewise.

I have two large boxes in the barn of alphabetically filed letters sent by people who reported to us on their progress in homesteading. Some were defeated; others, successful. I retained their letters, thinking someone could someday use them in an interesting thesis on homesteading enthusiasms of the time.

Our place was becoming known and we were also visited by newspaper, magazine, radio, and TV personages. This we did not need nor want, but interviewers often came. A video team turned up in the late 1970s to ask Scott's opinion on the energy crisis. "Come up with me to the woodpile," said Scott, "and I'll show you one way to solve it." He handed one man an axe for splitting, and to Roger Mudd, the interviewer, a double-handed saw, and they went to work to provide fuel for at least one family.

On another occasion, after publication of *Continuing the Good Life* in 1979, two carloads of CBS cameramen came to the farm for an interview on the Good Life in Maine. Scott was down on the beach, in working clothes, forking seaweed into his pickup truck. "Hey, fella," they called out. "Where is the Nearing place?" "Up the road to the left," Scott gestured and went on to finish his work. They found me, the lady of the house, at home and were told the man they sought was down on the beach gathering seaweed. Down to the beach they hustled with their gear, to try to catch him at his work.

I remembered a parallel story of an old man who was working at a stone wall. A pompously important gentleman drew up and inquired, "Can you tell me where the poet Joaquin Miller lives?" "Up there," replied the old man, pointing. The visitor stepped down and pulled out a half dollar. "Here, hold my horses for me, my good man." Twenty minutes later, the gentleman, who had spent an unhappy time puffing up the steep mountain road, came down, red-faced, and drove off quietly. Joaquin Miller went on building the wall.

Here is one written comment on "visiting the Nearings" by Professor Ronald LaConte, when he first dropped by in 1980:

> In an age in which information passes for knowledge and knowledge often masquerades as wisdom, a meeting with a genuinely wise human being is indeed a strange encounter—of the valuable kind—and Scott Nearing is unquestionably a wise man.
>
> It is not merely his years that earn him this description. Nor is it his accumulated knowledge, which is formidable. No, wisdom exists in the beneficial application of knowledge, not merely in the knowing but in the knowing why you know. To visit with the Nearings is to see knowledge applied not only beneficially but gracefully.
>
> In the house, the outbuildings, the gardens—everywhere, there is the beauty of both form and function. Things not only work, they work in harmony and they look good. This is the essence of wisdom.
>
> To sit and talk with Scott, whose life has spanned almost a century, is to be reminded that there are constants, that beyond today's computer games and television sets are natural rhythms and human values that do endure. A visit with the Nearings is a reminder that there are other things to plug into.

We kept open house in other ways. In Vermont we had had Sunday morning music meetings. On our Sunday evenings in Maine, classical records were played or visiting artists performed. Anyone was welcome to attend. Monday evenings were more political. Scott talked about current affairs and there were general discussions among the visitors and others who dropped by.

I formed friendships with three old ladies in the village of Harborside: Alice Gray, Carrie Gray, and Lois Blake, all widows I stopped in to see on my weekly trips to the post office. I brought them lettuces and sweet peas from the garden and blocks of maple sugar we had made in Vermont.

Jarvis Green was another newfound friend. He was our next-door neighbor who lived in a derelict house a mile or so up the road. He was bearded and unkempt, very sloppily dressed, with clothes never buttoned correctly. He was not too steady on his feet and lurched when he walked. He apparently lived on doughnuts and pie which he bought from his scant pension savings. I often asked him to stay for a meal when he dropped in to inquire how we were. He was courtly and polite, and said, "Thank you, I've had an ample sufficiency," after he had consumed the nourishing vegetables I piled high in his bowl.

I would take him to town for groceries if I met him on the road. I drove him to Blue Hill to a special stereopticon showing of slides of the neighborhood, which I thought would entertain him. It did, but his loud, uncouth voice and his disheveled appearance horrified the stylish people in the audience and we had a circle of empty seats around us. "Helen," I was warned, "Don't go around so much with that dirty man. People will think he's Mr. Nearing."

Jarvis had a dependent friend of his own, Miles Gray, a blind man, whom Jarvis shepherded around, taking him down to the beach and watching solicitously as his friend paddled about.

Jarvis died while we were away one winter. On our return we smoothed the bare gravesite, covered it with compost and planted catnip on it as he had liked cats. Perhaps it might bring him feline visitors, I thought. I chiseled his name, birthdate, and death date on a smooth rock we brought from his own dooryard and placed it in the cemetery.

In Maine I was able to find time to get back to my violin. I played in local affairs and combined with new friends in the nearby town to form a trio. I practiced long hours in the big sunny living room, watching Scott dig a pond in the back of the house while I did scales and exercises. Although in tying up with him I had put the possibility of a musical career behind me, I continued playing. Music was second to my work with him; I never at any time regretted this. The world is full of good violinists, and I listened to them on records and in concerts at nearby Bangor and Blue Hill where I went often to hear orchestral and chamber music.

I not only took part in classical music performances, I rollicked through easy pieces (what I called "ferry-boat music") with a neighboring family on the other side of the cape. These were evening diversions in the off-farming months. So I had music in my soul, if no longer on skilled fingertips, and solid productive outdoor work with a congenial partner—ensuring a good and complete life.

Outdoor work was Scott's recreation. The pond he dug had originally been a swamp. He visualized a place to swim, a source of water to be piped onto the garden, and a safeguard in case of fire. Instead of calling for a bulldozer he decided to dig it himself, and that he did with a wheelbarrow, shovel, and pickaxe. He took out fourteen thousand loads of good rich muck to enrich the garden soil and compost piles. Even after having done nine-tenths of the work on it himself he always called it "our" pond on which "we" had worked, whereas I had done little or nothing to it.

We did some rebuilding on the old wooden house, putting in a fireplace and chimney, adding a balcony for sleeping out and for my yodeling, which I had learned in the Austrian Tirol. Our largest venture was putting a stone wall around our one-hundred-square-foot garden. This took fourteen years to finish as it was a spare-time job and done in off moments. We enjoyed working at it and saved it for recreation, instead of golf or tennis. The wall was five feet high and three or four into the ground, serving to keep out rabbits, woodchucks, dogs, and deer as well as weeds and slugs from the neighboring lawn.

The last building we put up together was in fact "Helen's house." I designed the house and chose its location directly overlooking the bay. I laid every stone in it myself, allowing Scott to hand me shovels full of concrete he mixed in a wheelbarrow. The big living room and the adjacent study had flagstone floors that we laid ourselves. All through the house, walls were paneled with pine locally obtained. The interior was simply furnished, most of the chairs and tables homemade. Wood stoves heated the house and of course wood was used for cooking.

Back of this house we also put up a five-foot-high stone wall around a smaller fifty-by-fifty garden space, with a solar greenhouse which again provided us with greens long through the cold New England winter.

Designing and building the home we had lived in in Vermont for nineteen years and this stone house in Maine were surprising features of my life. Where had I learned the capacities of an architect, of a builder, and of a stone mason? Yet the two broad-roofed, balconied, many-windowed, stone-floored domiciles were aspects of myself—my larger being, my skin, my shell. I stained their pine-paneled, book-lined walls, adding antique Japanese prints and some of my mother's paintings. A hand-carved plaque with emblems of all the world's religions and the insignia "There Is No Religion Higher Than Truth" had been commissioned by my father for the Ridgewood house. It had been moved from there to Vermont and thence to the Maine living room. On a staircase timber leading to the bedrooms, I carved the names of my favorite things: "Sunshine . . . Birdsong . . . Snowfall . . . Trees." Where had I learned these arts of decoration? No one, including myself, knew.

"There is some of the same fitness in a man's building his own house," wrote Thoreau in *Walden*, "that there is in a bird's building its own nest. Who knows but if men constructed their dwellings with their own hands, and provided food for themselves and families simply and honestly enough, the poetic faculty would be universally developed, as birds universally sing when they are so engaged. But alas! we do like cow-birds and cuckoos, which lay their eggs in nests which other birds have built. . . ."

Scott must have had low periods, dismays and misgivings and self-questionings in his life, but he rarely mentioned them in public or private. I once asked if he regretted the large decisions he had made in his life, which cut him off from publishing opportunities, from political associations, and from an enjoyable and successful teaching career, changing his life so fundamentally. He took my question seriously and pondered it. "No," he said. "I would act much the same if I had to do it over again, even knowing the results of my actions and decisions. Perhaps I would be even stronger in my attitudes. But in my personal relations I would try to do better. There I hope I have learned." Perhaps he was thinking about his relations with his first wife, Nellie Seeds, and with his son John, with whom he had wide political differences.

The Seeds family had been neighbors of Scott's in Philadelphia in the early days. Nellie attended Bryn Mawr as well as the University of Pennsylvania and graduated with two doctorates. In 1908, a few years after their marriage, they collaborated on a book, *Women and Social Progress*, and she stood by him during the stressful years in Philadelphia and Toledo when he was ousted from his university posts. But they separated some years before I met him when she apparently decided that she preferred a less stringent life-style. His distaste for the usual bourgeois comfortable way of living became so strong that he eventually rebelled and acquired a wooden bowl and spoon and chopsticks and used them at the family table. His outstandingly obstinate behavior (much like Tolstoy's), and his espousal of vegetarianism, became a raw point in family relations. The two boys, John and Bob, sided with their mother and often derided Scott's eccentricities.

Robert, the younger boy, was a sunny convivial child who got along with everybody. He never developed strong opinions on either side of the political spectrum. He remained fond of and close to both parents despite their differences. He was a family man par excellence and would have liked the family to stay together.

But from boyhood, John struck a differing stance from his father. While Scott was being attacked in the press and in the universities for his antimilitary stand during the First World War, John, as a little boy, was selling war bonds, saying proudly "My father is a pacifist; I am a militarifist." In college, John officially changed his name from "John Scott Nearing" to "John Scott." His father thought it a good idea that he stood on his own feet, neither advantaged nor disadvantaged by his parent's name.

In his early twenties, while he was at the University of Wisconsin, John assumed the role of a flaming radical and termed his father a "liberal pinko." He dropped out of college in 1931. Scott thought he should continue and finish the term, but John went to the Soviet Union in 1932 and took up welding in Magnitogorsk and attended the local university. He married a Russian fellow-student, Masha, and their two daughters, Elka and Linka, were born there. Later he went to Moscow to do some writing about his experiences. There he encountered American correspondents who were making a comfortable living sending articles back to the United States. Anti-Stalin stories and critical material on the Soviets were proving very profitable and there was money to be made out of them.

John became a correspondent himself, leaving the Soviet Union at times to get his stories past the censors. After sending some especially revelatory material he was evicted from the country with Masha and the children. Arriving in New York in 1941, he wrote denunciatory articles and spoke critically about life in the Urals and the whole Soviet situation. This was very acceptable to the American press and public. John was soon employed by Henry Luce and became successful on the lecture circuit.

Scott wrote to him in December 1949:

> There was a time when you saw yourself settling down in Madison, Wisconsin, or Ithaca, N.Y., living very simply, studying for a couple of years, completing your college credits and making yourself a specialist. Such a program might have produced significant results. Instead, you chose to buy a Lincoln car and built a mansion in Ridgefield, Connecticut. You are allying yourself with the top U.S. income group. This will mean, almost inevitably, red-baiting or mud-slinging, much as you did in your recent *Life* article. If you can do that shamelessly enough, Hearst and Luce may compete for your services.
>
> Ever since you said to me that you wanted to work with a big enterprise like Life-Time-Fortune in order to see how it operated, I replied that you might gain much needed experience but that there was a real danger of your being engulfed by the oligarchy. I have watched your course with increasing concern.
>
> One day you will wake up and see what you have done and are doing. I hope that the awakening may come in time for you to put a remnant of your own life to some constructive use and save the youngsters from a social environment which is shallow, false and frustrating.

In another letter Scott wrote:

You have chosen the reactionaries as your close associates in business, politics and social relationships. I have no way of knowing whether you agree with them, but whether you do or not, you are lined up with them and are promoting their cause.

This puts us on opposite sides of the cold civil war which is being waged in the U.S.A. and makes any relations, especially social ones, exceedingly difficult. I assume you regret this. I certainly do. But civil war is no respecter of family relationships. It is one of the outstanding facts of present-day life. I cannot go to Ridgefield as you suggest.

You live in a big house in a world filled with poorly housed people. Two-thirds of the human family are inadequately nourished; you will invite over-fed people and will over-feed them some more. Your guests will drink alcohol, smoke tobacco and eat meat. I am strongly opposed to all these practices. My presence might irritate the drinkers, smokers and carcass eaters, and if issues were raised, unpleasant situations might develop. My way of life is in such opposition to the life pattern of you and your guests that I feel it would be wiser for me not to be present. Life is filled with likenesses and differences. But differences often become so great as to make association uncomfortable and difficult. You will excuse me from attending.

In answer to a later letter from John he wrote:

Talk about "progressive Republicans" is like the talk of 'progressive Tsarism' from 1905 to 1907. You have left the ranks of the revolutionists, have moved into the center of world counter-revolution, and in effect allied yourself with the counter-revolution. This is true politically, in your writings, speeches and other political acts. It is true economically. You are drawing a salary from one of the most completely counter-revolutionary groups in the U.S. [the Luce publications]. You are taking pay as a lecturer for counter-revolutionary audiences.

It is also true socially. The place you have chosen to live is a comfortable nest in the smug suburbia of the world's counter-revolutionary center, New York City. You are bringing up your children in a bourgeois atmosphere. They, like you, live on the cream skimmed from the labor and blood of the masses. The last time I saw them they did not even know the word "cooperative" when I took them to the Co-op. "What is that?" they asked.

You may well imagine how keenly I regret not seeing Elka and Linka. Also how earnestly I hope that you and Masha will be unable to corrupt them by immersing them in the banal, stultifying life which you have chosen for yourselves and for them. But they must stand on their own feet, and if they are unable to resist the snares with which you have decided to surround them, they are unworthy to play a part in building a better world.

John sought and accepted a position with Radio Free America, broadcasting American-oriented news to the Soviet Union. At that point Scott wrote him:

You have made your position quite clear. You are now one of the official handimen of the U.S. Establishment. This broad umbrella is held up by the industrial-military complex, plus the communication media. On its record since 1945 the Establishment had been the financier, armorer and spokesman for wealth and privilege all over the planet. You are now officially engaged as one of the policy shapers of the Establishment. Your leadership includes the galaxy of double-talkers, double-dealers, liars, robbers and murderers presently entrenched in Washington. Any victory for this outfit is a disaster for mankind, especially for the young men who will be drafted to fight its wars. You have been working under the direction of these reactionaries for years. I have been sorry to see you take this job among their dupes and stooges.

I wish you might have chosen differently. But you made your real decision when you bought in Ridgefield, and the rest followed. I regret this more than I can say. But you have decided to take this important position. I have no choice but to make the issue personal as well as political. One cannot run with the hare and attack with the hounds. My side has been chosen and followed for years. Your recent political act has placed us on two sides in a formidable, and for many of us, fatal struggle. So it is, and by your choice.

It may be wondered why only Scott's letters and none of John's are given here. Scott wrote by hand and I often made typewritten copies of those I thought significant. Scott continued his decades-long practice of destroying all his incoming mail.

Here is a note Scott sent Masha in response to one from her:

> You wrote about John's recent letter to me and asked me to answer it.
>
> You know of course, that in the last few years the government of the U.S.A. has fallen into the hands of a gang of law-breaking lawyers, whose titular leader was and is Richard Nixon.
>
> Internally, as shown by the Watergate investigation, and internationally, through the C.I.A., this gang has ignored the Constitution, broken United States law, violated treaties, filled its own pockets out of the public treasury, arranged for assassinations, waged undeclared and illegal wars. One of the chief tasks of this gang of outlaws has been suppression of socialism-communism.
>
> John has chosen to associate himself officially with this gang and assist in the operation of its criminal and counter-revolutionary activities. Need I say that I am sad and ashamed beyond words at this latest of John's moves into this gang of reaction and counter-revolution.
>
> So long as he continues on this line, his path and mine will be quite separate. John is neither soft-headed nor inexperienced. He has deliberately chosen his course. I wish it were otherwise, but he is master of his own life.

In a letter to a friend who questioned Scott's sharp con-
demnation of his son, he wrote:

> I cannot associate myself with someone in his line of work. I
> am sorry. He is committed to counter-revolution under the aus-
> pices of the U.S. government. I want nothing to do with him.
> There are personal obligations that sink to unimportance, and so-
> cial obligations that are paramount. John knows better. He is try-
> ing to overthrow the only effort being made to build up a better
> form of life style than civilization. I'm ashamed of him and hor-
> rified at what he is doing. With his background he knows better;
> he is on the other side of the barricades and is to be treated as
> such. As long as he is in his present job he is working against ev-
> erything I am working for.

Then Scott cited the Roman judge who had to sentence to
execution his own son as a looter, and who sadly did so.

While on a lecture tour in December 1976, at the age of
seventy-one, John Scott died of a heart attack in a Chicago
hotel. Scott did not attend the funeral, writing Elka:

> Thank you for sending me a wire about John's passing. He
> has been a sick man for a long time, due to bad diet and an un-
> hygienic life. That can be maintained for a few years but sooner
> or later it takes its toll.
>
> As you know, I disagreed with John for years. When he re-
> tired from the Luce empire and took a job under Nixon's gang, I
> rebelled. I do not have to tolerate official counter-revolution. I
> am sorry, of course. Up to a certain point I was neutral and said
> as little as possible. Latterly I have repudiated his course in life
> and am still doing so. I will not attend the funeral if one is held. I
> am writing Masha words of sympathy and encouragement. She is
> a stranger in a strange land. I wish her well.

To his son Bob he wrote:

Elka sent me a wire today about John. I am sorry—especially for John, who wasted a big section of his life on Henry Luce and Co., destroyed his own health and had little enough to show for it except a few filthy depreciated dollars and a batch of non-productive real estate. Too bad! He was an able chap. I wish we might have had more with his talents. I am sorry not to go to Johnny's funeral. I not only disagreed with him but I resented and repudiated his role in the U.S.A. counter-revolution.

This must have been a sad sore spot for Scott throughout most of his life. Here is a scrap of paper dated November 24, 1911, from his files:

As I searched the joyous grey eyes, I realized that the life of this six-year-old boy would be shaped by three things: 1. the qualities which came by heredity from his parents; 2. the attitude of society, in the home, the school, the playground and the workshop; 3. the decisions which he makes in his own soul. Fathers and Mothers, what have you dared? Society, will you raise him up, or smite him? My child, what will you decide? Consider well these things, for it is the future which waits expectant for your answers.

In a notation to himself, filed under "Writing: An Old Man's Legacy," Scott wrote in 1946 what seemed to pertain to John.

You who are younger have no idea how we who are older yearn to make good our sins and blunders and to fill our warped and wasted lives through those that are kin to us. We watch them from near and from far. If we are short-sighted we try to influence their judgements. We suffer in their frustrations and rejoice in their triumphs. Perhaps such experiences are most keenly felt by parents for their children and grandparents for their grandchildren. At the same time there is not a sincere teacher or counsellor who does not strive unceasingly to arouse his young charges to exert their full powers.

My relations with *my* parents continued to be warm and close through those years, although for some time they had deplored my relationship with Scott. Finally, in the 1940s, I was able to persuade them to come up for several summers from Florida where they had settled into a pleasant college town. I had not changed my objectives or my way of living, but they had come to realize my deep commitment and dedication to serious purposes—and to Scott.

They respected our intent and perseverance, although without agreeing with our politics. They mellowed with personal contact and grew to appreciate and love Scott. It was a real satisfaction for me that they finally overcame their previous prejudices and objections.

It was soon after moving to Maine that we initiated a new activity which had not been possible when we were busy sugaring in Vermont. Deprived of the opportunity of teaching youth in established institutions, Scott wanted to try free-lance lecturing, gypsying around the country by car. As Chaucer put it: "Gladly wolde he lerne, and gladly teche," in or out of school. We planned to take annual educational excursions in winter through the country, visiting every state in the Union. The purpose would be to hold meetings where possible; to distribute our books and pamphlets; to get a chance to evaluate public opinion, and to see local conditions. I made the arrangements with town and city groups, schools and private householders, scheduling dates and sending out publicity. Churches, ethical societies, Jewish forums, community centers, and student groups responded with invitations as did private householders.

We bought a secondhand station wagon which we loaded down with books to sell and literature to distribute. We took three winter trips—in 1952, 1953, and 1954—driving thousands of miles from the East Coast to the West, over the North and far into the South. Attendance at public and private gatherings varied from ten people to fifty to five hundred. There were occasional overflow meetings, particularly of students in college towns, and once, in Oklahoma, only one person attended, the hostess herself. She had cleared her living room, spread refreshments, and no one came—frightened apparently by the residual McCarthy pressures of the time.

In some towns we were turned away from prearranged homes where we were to stay. Such radical visitors were questionable. One frightened housewife peeked out the kitchen window while her husband came to the door and handed Scott a ten-dollar bill. "Go to the nearest motel," he said. "My wife won't have you." At another home where we were supposed to stay, a former radical friend of Scott's said, "My daughter wants to go to the junior prom. Something said at mealtime might offend her new young man." The atmosphere throughout the country was wary and cowardly.

There was widespread opposition voiced at our meetings against any escalation of the war in Korea, although Gallup polls showed about two-thirds of those questioned throughout the country supported the president. In all of our meetings active discussion was carried on by young and old in favor of peace.

Sometimes collections were taken up and payments made; at other times expenses were barely covered. Profits on the trips were rare, but our aims were accomplished: ideas and literature were made available and general public opinions were evaluated.

One year Scott spoke at the Community Church of Boston, the Ethical Society of Philadelphia, three meetings at the Miami Beach Forum, with no large meetings between Florida and California, a distance of about three thousand miles. There were meetings in San Francisco; in San Jose and Carmel and at the Westside Jewish Community Center in Los Angeles, and five meetings at the Unitarian Church of Los Angeles. Other trips covered the northwestern states into British Columbia, Vancouver, and Victoria, and back east through the northern states.

Introducing Scott in the winter of 1954, Stephen Fritchman, the minister of the First Los Angeles Unitarian Church, said:

> Scott Nearing is a symbol to me and thousands around the world—a symbol of the ability of a human being to shatter the utter nonsense about the generation gap—the absurdity of the cultivated synthetic myth that only youth can be joyous or growing.
>
> Scott Nearing, like Casals, Picasso, and the late Dubois, is a vital, alert, unintimidated leader of men and women of all ages, all races, all nationalities. He has shaped a philosophy and a discipline for living, and what is more, he has practiced it.
>
> I have read his writings and heard him speak for thirty years or more, and found him always compelling me to pull up my intellectual socks, to reexamine my most basic ideas, and most of all, to try harder to make my professions and my actions jibe better.
>
> To me, as to thousands, he has been a merciless, lovable, provocative, suggestive prophet of righteousness, an exemplar of common sense in living and of courage to use that seventy percent of the brain most people let rot unused, and to exercise that ninety-eight percent of the conscience which most people do not exercise at all.
>
> In this new day of the toad, this time of babbling fools in high places, of idiot misleaders with their fingers in the public jam pot and their consciences in the deep freeze, because of Scott Nearing we should all be a little more courageous as we face the world today.

No teacher I ever knew and honored did more for me than Scott Nearing—to sharpen my fuzzy mind, my emerging conscience, my moral self-confidence, my muddled politics. He helped make a humanist of me; he helped make a socialist of me. I want to be around to say this all over again on his one hundredth birthday.

A young woman graduate of the University of Pennsylvania wrote:

> To me, Scott's most outstanding characteristic is his ability to respond promptly and constructively to whatever challenges life presents him, whether they are personal, societal, or universal. His strength comes, I think, from his ability to integrate all aspects of his life into a unified whole, which allows him to think and live simply and genuinely, according to the truth as he sees it.

The governor of Maine, Kenneth M. Curtis, in giving Scott an award on November 19, 1971, from the State of Maine Commission on the Arts and Humanities, said:

> History is replete with examples of men of vision who, like Thoreau, listened to the beat of a different drummer and who were destined to wait for a laggard world to come abreast of their doctrines and heed their warnings. Such a prophet is with us today. Long before any of us were born, this man was doing battle. He spoke out against child labor, against war; he predicted the decay of great cities, the pollution of air and waters, the decline of personal independence. Economist, environmentalist, sociologist, lecturer and writer, he prescribed the good life and practiced what he preached. In our State of Maine, on Penobscot Bay, his doors are open to the hundreds of people who come each year to learn the secrets of living off the land, and yet, within that rigorous discipline, he finds the energy and leisure for writing, for music, and for civic affairs. Clearly, this man has made an art of his life.

A year earlier *World Tomorrow* magazine had declared:

> For thousands in the radical movement, whatever their politics, he will continue to be an inspiration as a teacher, not through his propaganda so much as through his rare qualities of rigid honesty, a lovable selflessness, and the essential integrity of the contradictory virtues which make up his character. . . . In the field of social science we need go no further than Thorstein Veblen and Scott Nearing for illustration of master minds "cribbed, cabined, and confined" by an unappreciative generation, while platitudinous nonentities fill the outstanding places in the realm of sociology, economics, and politics.

So, we made a dent with our cross-country trips. Scott's lifetime accomplishments were recognized: economist, educator, pacifist, civil rights champion, leftist politician, international socialist, ecologist, back-to-the-lander, futurist. He made a large contribution in all these fields, no doubt adding more to the general welfare than if he had stayed in academia. One correspondent wrote him: "You should have no regrets about having given up the life of the academic teacher. In fact, you have taught many more people than one usually reaches during an academic career."

This opinion is reflected in a letter written to Scott by Lucien Price, an editor of the *Boston Globe*, who told him of a boy who was impressed "powerfully" by meeting Scott. "This is all an old story to you, and I suppose has long since ceased to even interest you, but the effect of your mere personality and position on this youngster was one of the experiences of his life. He volleyed questions at me for another hour after we drove out of your yard and was busy setting his thoughts to rights for the next two days.

"To me it was very touching to see what effect a thoroughly integrated life could have on a young man who still has that job to do for himself without a word having been said on the subject.

"The visit was a keen enjoyment to me and I shall think about it a good deal. It has struck me that this phase of your life may prove to have been quite as useful as any other, and possibly even more so." He quoted from *The Education of Henry Adams*: "A teacher affects eternity; he can never tell where his influence stops."

When at home in Maine after our travels, we settled down to read and write. Together we produced three books about our travels: *USA Today: Educational Excursions through Darkest America* (1955); *The Brave New World* (1958), on Russia and China; and *Socialists around the World* (1958), a report written for *Monthly Review*. We also wrote the book Pearl Buck had suggested on our life in Vermont, *Living the Good Life* (1954); a pamphlet on *The Right to Travel* (1959); and, eventually, a book on year-round gardening in a cold climate, *Our Sun-Heated Greenhouse* (1977), and *Continuing the Good Life* (1979), which rounded out our half century of homesteading with an account of the new farm in Maine. In the 1960s and 1970s, we wrote a regular column in *The Mother Earth News*.

I started up on my own and got out a *Good Life Picture Album* (1977) with photographs of our lives together and apart; a vegetarian cookbook called *Simple Food for the Good Life* (1980); an anthology of *Wise Words on the Good Life* (1980); and a large picture book describing, step by step, *Our Home Made of Stone: Building in our 70s and 90s* (1983).

Scott incorporated the name Social Science Institute as an imprint for the books we had to publish ourselves. It was chartered under the laws of Maine in 1954 as a nonprofit educational entity to publish books and hold classes or seminars on social science. It never evolved into his hoped-for effective action and research organization on international peace studies and the social sciences, but still fulfills other purposes—helping to maintain the farmstead as a modest model of home building, functional independence, of simplicity and right-livelihood on the land. This model includes human, social, and natural ecology, organic gardening, and community participation. The institute sells and distributes books, holds workshops, and keeps open house as a Good Life Center for visitors and students.

Occasionally, Scott was asked to write articles. In the 1960s a new magazine, called *The Minority of One*, was starting up. Upon being asked by the editor to contribute, Scott wrote the following letter:

> In the social desert which we call the United States of North America any oasis refreshes. For a long time, Henry Geiger in *Manas*, and latterly you, in *The Minority of One*, have been pouring waters of moral and intellectual integrity on the desert sands of U.S.A. readership. You have taken on the herculean task of editing a magazine on moral and social protest and publishing it without soliciting or accepting the profiteer-subsidy or advertising. Henry Geiger also goes it alone and supports *Manas* by running a printing plant. I respect and honor both of you for getting out your magazines under prevailing U.S.A. conditions.
>
> Thank you for asking me to write for *TMO*. That brings up the question: Can I make a contribution acceptable to your magazine and its readers? If there is a chance that I can do so I would like to try.
>
> I have five major social concerns: (1) the ability of the human race to make a sustained effort to provide a good life for all. Lenin asserted this possibility. Spengler questioned it; (2) the capacity of homo sapiens to use technology for production and

construction and at the same time prevent the destructive minority of mankind from using technology for self-extinction; (3) can the institutions of civilization be made to contribute more than they detract from the good life; (4) can social science and social engineering be made a major field of endeavor for the efforts of aspiring youth; (5) the role of the U.S.A. oligarchy in the drama of western civilization.

At my age and with my background I am not likely to stray far afield from these and similar concerns. Do you think that they might contribute to the purposes which you have in mind for *The Minority of One?*

The magazine folded before such a working relationship could be established.

Invitations came to Scott to speak at various international peace conferences. He attended whenever possible; going to Russia, to Sri Lanka, and several times to South America. Some of his letters to me contained personal accounts of his living conditions and some were reports on his talks.

In traveling he continued to avoid stylish hotels and only rarely entered restaurants. Here is a letter he wrote me from São Paulo when he was traveling through South America in 1963.

I came here last night from Montevideo. We got into the city from the airport about 10:00 P.M. At the airport they directed me to "Hotel Excelsior." It turned out to be a twenty-story commercial hotel, U.S.A. style. I took one look at it and never went inside; just picked up my bags and started to look about. I tried three small hotels, all full. Finally I found a tiny one on a rather noisy square. It had running cold water, no heat, two straight chairs and a good table; toilet nearby and very clean. For this I pay eight-hundred cruzieros, about $1.50, with breakfast. Across the street is a fruit store. This morning, for my other meals, I bought two pounds of grapes, four large persimmons and two fair-sized avocados—all for fifty U.S.A. cents. The fruit here is excellent and seems abundant. There are numbers of handcarts in the streets, laden with bananas. I have not yet priced or tasted them. If I stayed here I could live for $2.50 or $3.00 a day and live very well.

On the same trip he wrote me a note from Rio de Janiero:

In this hotel I am paying three-thousand cruzieros ($4.80) a day for a fine room and splendid breakfast. This is about all the monthly wages of a local farm laborer. So I will move.

And from Venezuela he wrote:

Our meeting at Caracas University was quite an event. The people who arranged it were not sure it would draw, so they apologized in advance for the probable small crowd. They decided to use a classroom that seated 100 instead of the auditorium. At 10 minutes to 8 when the meeting was to start, every seat was taken and about 100 more people were still crowding into the room.

I wrote a rather detailed outline of the talk, interlined by the translator in Spanish, on a long blackboard in the front of the room. The Chairman, head of the Social Science Department, introduced the topic: Economic Crises in the United States. All went well for a translated sentence-by-sentence talk. There were questions at the end, the first one being: "Could the U.S. alone solve the problems of the under-developed countries?" My answer was "No, you people must do it yourselves." The second question: "You have described the crisis in the U.S.A. but you have no remedy. Could you suggest a remedy in a couple of words, in two sharp words?" "Yes," I answered, "I can. The two sharp words are Social Revolution."

Pandemonium broke loose. The students stamped, shouted and applauded. The demonstration broke out in the up-to-now quiet room like a pistol shot. I was utterly astonished. It was several minutes before quiet was restored. By this time the room was packed with students sitting on the floor and standing and there were heads in the windows. They kept pushing in through the doors that opened into the corridor.

More questions followed and I enlarged on the subject of basic change to a socialist North and South America. One student asked about the Cuban situation: Had I been there and what could I say about it. After some discussion on Cuba another student asked what I would suggest the people in Venezuela should do. I said, "The Cuban people did not ask me that question; they knew what to do and are going on with the business in hand." Again a roar of applause and demonstration that lasted several minutes. Finally the Chairman thought it time to adjourn the meeting. The whole thing reminded me of student meetings in the U.S.A. in the early 1920s. For me and seemingly for the students it was a memorable affair.

A different reception awaited him when he addressed a class of young Americans in Chicago that same year. Scott wrote me:

> Maynard Krieger asked me to go to the university and talk with some of his students. I expected about ten or twelve people. There were about two-hundred-fifty, I guess, but I went ahead as we planned, with a fifteen minute statement followed by forty minutes of questions. On the blackboard I put:

Ruling Class Project:
Exploitation

Technique	Result
1. Accumulation of things	1. Bondage to them
2. Soma Juice	2. Oblivion
3. Get by	3. Corruption & decay

and across from it I wrote:

Libertarian Counter-Project:
Emancipation

Technique	Result
1. Frugality	1. Self-reliance
2. Asceticism	2. Conservation of energy
3. Planned purpose	3. Growth

I told them that the Ruling Class Project was a formula used today in a system that was ugly and tawdry and enslaved them. I said the only real freedom exists in the minimizing of needs.

The reaction of the students was fierce. They simply would not give up their beer, their cigarettes, and their comforts. Participation in joint activity and self-discipline, which are necessary for the next step, was completely beyond them. Apparently everyone is not capable of coordinated purpose.

He might have repeated a favorite rhyme of his:

> Dollars and dimes! Dollars and dimes!
> To be without money is the worst of all crimes.
> To grab what you want, and keep all you can
> Is the first and the last and whole duty of man.

Or another favorite saying of his: "The iron chains struck off, behold, men fight to put on chains of gold." And to illustrate the counter-project he might have quoted William James: "Lives based on having are less free than lives based on either doing or being."

Within days of his talk at the Caracas University, Scott was deported back to the United States as a dangerous man. This appraisal was underlined by Leo Huberman, editor of *Monthly Review* magazine, who introduced Scott at a New York meeting after his return.

The man we are honoring tonight *is* dangerous. He has been thrown into prison, and out of many cities . . . in this country and abroad.

What makes him so dangerous in the eyes of the authorities? Does he go about armed, preaching violence? No, he doesn't carry a gun; he is a pacifist. Is he a rabble-rouser who incites his listeners to violations of law and order? No, he speaks eloquently and often—but always with the voice of reason. Do his writings inflame the unwary untutored mind? That cannot be, because he writes as he speaks—as a scholar who has read widely, sifted the evidence, and recorded his findings in simple direct language.

Nevertheless, the ruling class in capitalist countries makes no mistake in regarding Scott Nearing as a dangerous man. He is a danger to their power and privilege. He endangers their rule because he is a social scientist who is unafraid. He puts the world under his microscope, examines it intently, and, unlike most social scientists, has the courage to report what he sees, no matter who is hurt by his findings, no matter what the danger to himself.

He preaches sanity in an insane world. That's why he's a dangerous man. And he has done his job of scientific analysis of the world's ills so well and so long that he has opened the eyes of many people all over the globe. His little candle throws its beams in near and remote places, in developed and underdeveloped countries, in universities here, in the jungle huts of Africa, the *favelas* of Brazil, the guerrilla hiding-places of Asia. The only other person I can think of with comparable influence in the training of many people in government in the newly liberated countries was Harold Laski. I am thankful I had the privilege of friendship with both of these extraordinarily gifted teachers.

One other important fact about Scott explains, I think, why we honor him tonight. In a corrupt society, he remains incorruptible; in a period when opportunism is the fashion, he remains a steadfast adherent to principle. It was Paul Valéry who said, "You must live as you think, or sooner or later you will think as you live."

It is because Scott lives as he thinks that those of us who have been indebted to him for so long regard him as a saint—a saint with brains. All honor to one of America's greatest men!

Queries and Comments

It is better to know some of the questions than all of the answers.

James Thurber

*I*NNUMERABLE LETTERS came to us daily during our homesteading years, with questions on anything from compost to communism; from "Do you use soap to wash your hair?" to "Do you believe in God?" Sometimes we felt like Dear Abby and sometimes like Father William in Lewis Carroll's *Alice in Wonderland*: "I have answered three questions and that is enough, . . . Do you think I can listen all day to such stuff?" Usually it was an interesting part of the day's writing to respond to so many people, old and young, on so many subjects, and to have the opportunity to stimulate and be stimulated in turns by the matters brought up.

Following are about two dozen answers to questions that came in the mail.

*

What are your common interests as a couple? [Few of our friends and associates shared them all.]
1. The political and social: leftist organizations, foreign languages, travel
2. The ecological: gardening, work in the woods, love of nature and animals

3. The artistic and aesthetic: literature, music, poetry, pictures
4. The cosmic and esoteric: philosophy, life and death, meditation
5. Research and study: in libraries and at home, books read and written together
6. Planning and building: of houses, outbuildings, and gardens
7. Simple food: vegetarian, organic, unprocessed
8. Health: exercise, diet, yoga, fasting

✳

To a woman who asked in the 1970s how we kept our marriage growing and intact in these days of easy splitting, I answered:

"We do not always agree, but I know the way his mind works and respect his opinions and actions, and he's had to make allowances for mine.

"We have our interests in common, and our varying interests. I respect his competence and he, mine. We grow along together and yet spread our wings in various directions.

"Scott is a trained economist and sociologist, a very set A-B-C-D, 1-2-3-4 person. I am a musician, interested in artistic things, a lightweight in comparison to him. I've had to adapt to him and he to me.

"We have a division of labor: I handle and run the house and he directs the garden and outside work. He helps with the inside work and I with the outside work. We are a cooperating team. In our joint enterprise on construction work, for instance building our latest stone house, I handle and place the rock and he mixes the concrete.

"We have separate economies and bank accounts, and handle our financial affairs independently of each other. On occasion we borrow and lend to each other, and have joint family accounts which I keep and present for settlement a couple of times a year.

"We have very different personalities: he a staunch Leo and I a wiggly fish. Somehow this strange partnership works and has for forty years. We intend to go on together."

∗

We were often asked questions on aging and health. We answered together and variously.

"Growing old is living on the descending arc of the cycle of life between earth and death. It has many advantages as well as the obvious disadvantages of diminishing physical capacities. One is over the hump; one has done more or less what one could; not much is expected any more. There are stages of youth, householder, philosopher, and hermit which are recognized in India. Youth is the period of learning how to live, studentship. Middle age includes the duties of the family man and social being, the worldly activist. The last stage is that of abstract thought and meditation, the hermit, the non-attached.

"As to health, a simple formula of our food is: it should be fresh; it should be whole; it should be unprocessed. We avoid highly refined foods. The nearer you come to this idea the better for your digestive apparatus and the better for your health. Two profound philosophers of note have given the same healthful hint for a long and happy life. Lin Yutang in his *Importance of Living* wrote: 'It is largely a matter of the movement of the bowels.' And Bertrand Russell, in speaking of health and longevity in his autobiography wrote 'I attribute my own happiness to defecating twice a day with unfailing regularity.' We might also note the following from Elbert Hubbard: 'If you have health, you probably will be happy, and if you have health and happiness, you will have all the wealth you need, even if not all you want.'

"Here are some factors for health and a long life which we

have put into practice: positive, optimistic thinking; a good conscience; outdoor exercise and deep breathing; no smoking; no alcohol or drugs, including coffee and tea; a simple diet—vegetarian, sugar-free, salt-free, low in calories and fat and 55% raw. These will vitalize the life span. Avoid medicines, doctors, hospitals."

※

To a girl who was discouraged with regard to her life-style:

"From what you write I gather you have come to a transfer point. Start all over again. Start anew—just as though you were born again. Forget the past, after learning all you can from it. Go to a new place. Get a job—the most congenial and satisfying you can find. Work at it regularly and steadily.

"This will give you confidence and enable you to learn to live by taking full charge of yourself and your affairs.

"Perhaps you can arrange to help someone. This will allow you to forget your own troubles. You are too valuable a person to waste your time in moping, recriminations and self-pity. Get on to the job you came here to do and do it with all of your might and to the best of your ability.

"Love, good cheer, and a good life. Scott"

I dug out this quotation from Frank Townshend's *Earth* and sent it to the girl: "If you are discontented or depressed it is because you are out of harmony with the world you live in. That world you cannot greatly alter. Yet by as much as you are able to grow into harmony with your surroundings, so will your pain grow less. The only thing you can alter is yourself."

And I found her a rhyme, written in 1750 by John Wesley, the itinerant divine:

Do all the good you can,
By all the means you can,
In all the ways you can,

In all the places you can,
At all the times you can,
To all the people you can,
As long as ever you can.

❋

We offered tips on de-stressing one's life:
1. Do the best you can, whatever arises
2. Be at peace with yourself
3. Find a job you enjoy
4. Live in simple conditions: housing, food, clothing;
   get rid of clutter
5. Contact nature every day; feel the earth under your feet
6. Take physical exercise through hard work; through
   gardening or walking
7. Don't worry; live one day at a time
8. Share something every day with someone else; if you
   live alone, write someone; give something away;
   help someone else somehow
9. Take time to wonder at life and the world; see
   some humor in life where you can
10. Observe the one life in all things
11. Be kind to the creatures

❋

Scott wrote this to a disheartened soul:
"There are four limitations on your enjoyment of a full, rewarding life. The first is the ability to live: that is, the sturdiness
of your body, your fund of energy, your emotional balance, the
keenness of your mind, the range of your intuitions, the clarity
of your vision. The second is the wisdom with which you
choose between various lines of conduct. The third is the extent to which you can live according to these choices. The

fourth is the stimulus to exquisite living that you can experience from the beauty of nature."

✻

To another discouraged and disgusted soul:

"You can put your conscience to sleep with the cheap abundant stimulants and depressants so generously and profitably provided by the U.S.A. ruling class. Having drugged your finer senses, you can do as everyone else does, say what everyone else says and wait humbly for the deluge.

"You can join the liberals, yap at the Soviet Union, at social planning, collective action, the working masses, talk endlessly, and grow bitter and cynical as a result of the frustration which aspiration without fulfillment and talk without action always bring.

"The human race has survived a long time. In science, the arts, philosophy and its numerous crafts, it has many items to its credit. Man seems to possess an almost infinite capacity to grow, develop and evolve. So let us take courage, keep our faith in the future and lend a hand in the present. Good cheer!"

✻

To a South American correspondent:

"You are one of the very many people who are bewildered, confused and not a little dismayed by the rush and surge of the changes that are buffeting and battering you in the whirlpool of the Great Revolution. It began around 1750; it has changed politics, communication, industry, science, the arts. In fact, it has created what is essentially a new world.

"The Great Revolution is still in full flood. If you are wise and foresighted (*a*) you will survive the crisis; (*b*) study it and understand it; (*c*) learn from it; and (*d*) if you are on your toes you will toss in your two-bits to help direct it.

"Up to a certain point in the process you will be confounded and confused. Beyond that point you will get hold of yourself and begin to play a part in directing the on-going social process. Get yourself in hand, become a self-conscious, self-directing, socially aware part of the whole big show which we call our expanding universe."

✳

A question came in on war and peace:

"I have your letter about peace candidates. The basis of our trouble is not war but the presence of a social system that produces war as surely as an apple tree produces apples. To be rid of war we must change (alter) the causes producing war. The warfare society is very old and well-rooted. 'There have always been wars and always will be' is the argument. After hearing Johnson talk peace while he wages war with napalm et al., a rational person would suspect political statements and promises."

✳

For a questioner who was wealthy:

"Affluence has its advantages. It takes off the pressures incident to scarcity and opens wide horizons. With a pocket full of money, one can go anywhere—including hell. We have no way of knowing what the results of affluence will be. Under the conditions prevailing in the United States it takes a strong person to formulate his own values of conduct and live up to them. It can be done, but is not easy. It is up to each of us to lead a disciplined, constructive life, and to lend a hand where possible. That is about it."

✳

Describing the opportunities and difficulties of homesteading in the spotlight in 1976:

"Last summer 1370 people visited Forest Farm. Maximum in any one day was thirty-two. On July 4 we had seventeen people to lunch. Most of the visitors were young. Many had read *Living the Good Life*. A good many were looking for land. A goodly proportion wanted to see a homestead in action. Many wanted to 'lend a hand' with the idea of learning how it operated. Most of our guests were very well-behaved. Some were good workers. Others were doing physical work for the first time. Quite a few wanted to stay—from a day to a year or so. A neighbor cut our hay on July 5. The next two days we raked by hand and stacked the hay. At one time we had eleven people working at the hay job, several too many for efficiency but everyone seemed to enjoy the work. We are also doing some stone building. On that job we can only handle five or six people effectively."

I added a postscript to Scott's accounting: "We're having literally thousands of visitors this summer. Rather a job to put up with such crowds. Twenty-six people for lunch last Saturday. By body count already fifteen hundred have come. I'm pretty pooped!"

※

Helen writing a hostess after a typical day on one of their western trips:

"What afternoon?
What day?
What town?

"You certainly warmed our hearts by your sudden appearance and your helpful instructions. I really was (and am) dizzy as the above dateline denotes, and couldn't figure out for a minute or two how we got here at all. Scott talks about this being a vacation trip, but it's hardly that! And he's done it year after year without a murmur. It really is strong men's work and

I can see why it's put the lines in his face and taken the hair from his head. And yet he remains the most vital and energetic chap I've met of his years, or half his years. This not to mention his high good humor.

"We ate your sweetly prepared lunch en route, arrived here at 2:30, called up the folks after parking in this motel and were told to 'come right over, the meeting has begun'! So we've hardly caught our breath. It is now 5:30 and I want to get this off before we go out *again*."

✳

From Scott to a young girl:

"Your New York shopping spree sounds as though you had been stocking up for a trip around the world. How do you think it would be if, instead of going into a store and coming out with clothes ready-made, you got the materials or even wove them yourself, and then made up your own clothes—perhaps with a little help from a relative or friend?

"Instead of sitting in movie houses, looking at pictures of something that rarely or never happens except in make-believe, you could spend your time out of school doing something that would test your imagination, develop skills, and give you a feeling of confidence in your ability to make useful and beautiful things.

"Worth thinking over, at any rate. It is not what we have but what we do that changes us and helps us grow. Often the things we have get in the way."

✳

To a woman in Lodi, California in the 1960s:

"You are right. The times are distressing, here and in other parts of the planet. Human beings have built up a 'grab-and-get' economy which is rough on all concerned. The alternative is 'share-and-share-alike,' which is unacceptable to those on top. As inflation grows, times will get harder. A lot of folks will die of hardships. Your safest bet is to produce and consume your own food. It would be easier for you than for us with our long hard winters. The point is to live a useful, good, harmless, productive life yourself."

✳

To a leftist comrade, also in the 1960s:

"The fragmenting of the Left in the U.S.A. is due in part to the super-individualism preached and practiced in this country. In part it is due to the carefully planned drive to destroy the Left as a political force.

"The youth revolt is a real mass movement, but lacking plan, discipline, organization. All of these will come with time and experience.

"I would guess that most of the young people who come under our influence will revert to their social background when they experience the real hardships that divergence from type almost inevitably involves.

"U.S.A. leadership is trying to build a world empire during a period when empires are unpopular and cost far more than they bring in. At the moment, the U.S.A. is bankrupting itself in this enterprise.

"The period through which we are living is stirring, challenging, and for many people, destructive. It is the downturn of a cycle of civilization. Less drastic than an earthquake, it lasts for generations or centuries, devastating and destroying.

"Rough weather ahead.

"It now seems pretty clear that U.S.A. armed personnel in Vietnam will be increased to more than half a million. Casualties will continue to rise. As yet, no war has been declared. L.B.J. & Company are therefore engaged in brigandage and piracy, and are handing the U.S.A. public an annual bill of twenty-five to thirty billion dollars to cover the cost of the adventure. Of course, it helps the economy, but it would be far cheaper in the long run to *give* the U.S.A. arms manufacturers twenty-five billion; save the lives being sacrificed in Vietnam and avoid the further loss of U.S.A.'s good name and goodwill all over the world."

❋

To a young girl who wrote and said she was graduating and "free at last":

"'Free' in this connection is rhetorical—nothing more. After graduation you will be at the mercy of

1. Your physical hungers, your undisciplined emotions, your errant mind, your vague aspirations and hopes. Above all, of your deeply embodied habit patterns which are yours and yours alone, and very tyrannical.
2. The frantic, hysterical pressures and counter-pressures of a social order in its death agonies.
3. The embracing and unfolding forces and influences of nature—of the universe of which you are a part.

"Unless you can be at peace with yourself, adjusted to the community and in balance with nature you will have a rough, unhappy and unrewarding life. You are free within physical limits: you can raise or not raise your own arm. But where others are concerned, once involved in relationships with others, your every act affects them and their actions affect you. Realize you are part of all that goes on around you."

⚜

To a colleague:

"Occasionally an impressive figure crossed our political horizon. None such is presently in sight. The Nixons, the Mc-

Governs et al., are no more responsible for our foreign policy than a conductor on a passenger train. The train operates on schedule; the conductor rides, calls the stations, collects the tickets. The train follows the rails.

"You take events here too personally. Over all they are quite impersonal. A potent leader might inject personality but no genius is in sight.

"Do not leave the country. Stick around. Pick a new train crew and maybe help remake the schedules. Eventually the tracks will have to be relaid, and on a new railbed.

"Neither the U.S. nor the universe is to be taken personally."

*

When people considered homesteading as a life-style they were warned that they must have inner resources as well as material resources. Their lives must have content. "A man who retires into solitude," said John Burroughs, "must have a capital of thought and experience to live upon, or his soul will perish of want." They must have goals and purposes in mind as well as money in the bank to purchase acreage.

*

There were some who wrote asking why there was no mention of religion in our books. There were attempts to convert us, and some people specifically asked if we believed in God. In 1980, answering one such questioner, Scott countered:

"In any serious discussion of a question such as yours 'Do you believe in God?' it is customary for the one who propounds the question to define the term. Before I answer your question, therefore, I would ask what you mean by God."

Answering a second time he wrote: "Thank you for your definition of God as 'the energy spirit that connects us all.' That is an unusual and interesting definition. I accept it with a slight change. Omit 'us,' making it 'the energy that connects all.' I suggest this because your definition as it stands seems to refer to human beings only. Taking out 'us' makes it easier to include animals, flowers, rocks, trees, and other aspects of the All. Using that as the definition, yes, I believe in the universe as it is, in all its aspects. I also believe that the universe changes a bit each hour and each day, so there is an ever-changing All. This makes possible an even shorter definition of the word 'God': 'All That Is.' This working makes God and Being mean essentially the same thing." (In this instance, his correspondent Paul Rifkin collected Scott's answer into his 1986 volume *The God Letters*.)

Helen wondered, Why use the word 'God'? We rarely do. Why not be content with 'the All-Being' or 'The Great Entirety'? Perhaps Empedocles said it best: 'The nature of God is a circle of which the center is everywhere and the circumference is nowhere.'"

✳

Helen wrote to a doctor friend who was interested in the state of their health after a long winter's trip, detailing their diet at that period:

"We finished a strenuous four-month winter's trip and landed back here in Maine late in February, both ten pounds overweight from bad food and bad living. Ignoring a cellar full of our good vegetables and fruits, we went on a ten-day apple diet (eating a dozen a day, whole or scraped) and lost more than ten pounds. We went about our everyday activities, which included a lot of work on accumulated printed matter and mail, but also tree cutting, sawing wood for our stoves, hauling logs, dragging huge rocks from an old stone wall over the ice to edge an island on our pond, and ice-skating. There weren't many days we weren't as or more active than any other people, young or old, on the Cape.

159

"We're now back on our regular diet of two cups of mint tea for breakfast; soup and cereals for lunch; salad and vegetables for supper. I've regained most of my ten pounds, but Scott (who does more outside work than I do, and harder) remains around the same weight. We're to bed by 10 and he's up by 5, doing most of his writing before breakfast and the activities of the day's jobs."

✳

To this same medical friend Scott wrote a letter later on:

"Thank you for your letter with concern on my health status. As I understand your proposal, you want me, each month, to furnish urine samples and have B-12 injections and other necessary medication and/or treatment.

"If I did this I would be trying to prolong my life under medical supervision for the rest of my life. Thank you, but I would rather die much earlier than follow such a course.

"My formula is to stay well and live as long as I can, in moderate health and vigor. If I cannot stay well by a normal diet and temperate living, the sooner I die, the better for me and the society of which I am a member."

✳

To a question on why we were vegetarians:

"For every possible reason, but primarily ethical. George Bernard Shaw always answered the same question by another: 'How can *you* justify the disgusting habit of consuming animal carcasses?' We know of no valid reason for eating flesh. The rotting carcasses are full of diseases and poisons. Raw fruits and vegetables and nuts are vital and clean if organically grown. A vegetarian diet is simpler, more economical, and kinder.

"Human beings make up only one form of life on the planet. There are many other forms: animal, vegetable, etc. Together they all make up the living pattern that exists interdependently on Earth. Each of these life forms is the expression of a force, including, presumably, a purpose. All are here to live, grow, develop and contribute. They live their own lives; they also live more or less together with other life forms. Mankind can harm them and use these fellow beings, enslaving them, buying and selling, working them, killing them and eating them. Mankind also uses them for experiments that may result in saving *human* lives.

"Our fellow creatures have as much right to live as we have. We would like to help them to live and develop—not hinder or harm them.

"You speak of 'pests' and the need to kill bugs, termites, flies, mosquitoes, and roaches; otherwise you fear they would very quickly take over the planet and make life impossible for humans. Are you aware that

1. Humans have destroyed countless forests, have overgrazed land and reduced it to uninhabitable deserts?
2. Humans have wiped out entire species of birds, fish and animals?
3. Humans slaughter wild animals for 'sport'?
4. That in historical times humans have deliberately destroyed the culture of other humans, have exploited them, enslaved them, and killed them by the tens of millions?
5. Have you travelled through the U.S.A. and seen the city slums, the hideous approaches to U.S.A. towns, the bill-boarded highways?

By any definition of 'pest,' in terms of 'live and let live,' human beings would surely take first prize."

※

We were asked our attitude to animals, to pets. I replied:

"The animals are our brothers; another nation living on earth, growing up beside us. They are not lesser beings; they are selves in different forms. Some of them have flippers, some wings for motivation; some have two propelling legs, some have four; we have only two. Some have thumbs, some have claws. We have manufactured claws and worse.

"We have no rights over these creatures; yet we exploit and imprison them. They should run wild and be on their own but we have corrupted them, enslaved them and modified their behavior and opportunities. Some of them like it, some don't. We have made friends of some and slaves of others.

"Scott was against having animal servitors or pets. 'Respect them. Let them run free,' he has said. My family always had pets: cats, dogs, canaries, parrots, chickens.

"There were only wild animals on the grounds in Vermont. In Maine a great white cat came with the place; he refused to leave it with the previous owner. (I did not say aloud that I would pay $100 extra for a place with such a cat!) Scott respected the animal because he was wild and free, far from domesticated. 'Whitey' had wintered alone for years before we came. From then on I had a succession of cats, all strays who came to the door in obvious need. Scott liked them and they him, but he disapproved in general of dependents. I loved anything with four legs and waving tail and furry ears and whiskers and pink noses and paws like pink raspberries, and especially their purring."

❋

We were asked about our use of machines: Scott disliked them and would gladly have done without any. We had a car, a truck, perforce. The latter was a necessity, living out in the wilds, far from town. It was also used to gather sand and gravel, rocks, lumber for building, wood for fuel, soil and seaweed and leaves for gardening. Chain saws and lawn mowers Scott abominated; the noise and stench offended him. He would rather work slowly and silently with handsaws and scythes and other manual tools.

Here is a letter he wrote in 1960 to an inquirer on the subject of gadgets, machines, automation, and the like:

"I am writing this letter by hand because I prefer that means of communication. I seldom use a typewriter, never a dictaphone. I do not want a mechanism between me and what I am trying to do on paper.

"When it comes to getting around, I always walk if possible. I use mechanical transportation reluctantly. I like to have my feet on the earth and move slowly enough so that I can observe and note what is going on about me.

"I do a great deal of physical work by hand. This morning I was stripping off sods with a mattock and piling them with a fork on a sod pile, then removing the underlying clay with a shovel and a wheelbarrow. A bulldozer would have done the same thing in 1/50th of the time. I might have stood and watched; but this morning I enjoyed every minute of the work and felt deprived when I was called to breakfast.

"I would not want to spend ten hours a day with a pick and shovel, but I enjoy a spot of vigorous physical exercise, especially if I can see a plan unfold and can see the results, in tangible form, of my own efforts. In this, as in all things, there are limits, beyond which we overdo. But my formula calls for the least necessary intervention between my purposes and plans and their execution. Life consists in doing, constructing, embodying ideas in form—not in pushing buttons."

❋

We were asked about meditation and yoga. People wondered whether I persisted in these practices once I became a farmer. I no longer did ritual exercises as such. Our daily lives involved constant exercising, lifting, bending, stretching, carrying, walking, swimming. If all were done with precision and focalization, all would be yoga in action.

Yes, we meditated—not always by sitting down cross-legged, trying to direct our erring thoughts toward higher realms. We might start the day with a recognition of our relationship with the whole, opening ourselves to an acknowledgment of the creative forces in the universe, keeping wide the channels of our being so that benign forces could stream through. We breathed especially deep of life at those times and tried to continue this sense of dedication throughout the day. Was this meditation? For us it was.

✽

We were asked why we did not have children and if we had, wouldn't that have affected our good life together.

I usually answered that it was bad enough at the time (fifty years ago) to live, unmarried, with a man; to have had illegitimate little Scotties and Scottinas around would have killed my devoted parents. They had had enough to bear as it was with my unconventional behavior. I said my life with Scott was so full that I had felt no lack, no incompleteness. This was proving an interesting life without children. It allowed us, too, to share everything more fully. In another incarnation we might have children together. I made a date with Scott for such an occasion in the future.

Meanwhile, we were surrounded with young people we could help on their way. Thousands of them have come through the years to our farms in New England to see us. Some stayed to live in the neighborhood and work with us, and others just visited, talked, and looked around. Countless youngsters wrote later how much they had been moved to modify their lives. Other thousands read our books on simple living and were influenced to a greater or less degree. Children we had aplenty. Besides, perhaps it was a contribution we could make to society—to keep down the population surge by not adding to it.

✻

There were many times we were considered too serious, too "square." Scott would not go to "parties" where there would be only drinks and chitchat. He despised them, although if someone needed help or work done, he was off in a minute. "I would only go if I could be useful" was usually his answer to invitations.

What do you do for recreation, for fun? we were often asked.

"Everything we do is recreation, is enjoyable, otherwise we wouldn't do it," we answered. As for "fun," it was not a word Scott used. Said William Blake in a letter to a friend: "Too much fun is of all things most loathsome. Mirth is better than fun, and happiness is better than mirth."

At one time I said as I was working on a book of my own, "I'm having a lot of fun with it, whether anyone else likes it or not." Scott remarked, not unkindly, "That's too bad you're having fun with it. Life is not about fun. Do a serious job at it."

It was only a cookbook, so it hardly got very serious.

Twilight and Evening Star

At the last, tenderly,
From the walls of the powerful fortress'd house,
From the clasp of the knitted locks, from the keep of the
*   well-closed doors,*
Let me be wafted.

Let me glide noiselessly forth;
With the key of softness unlock the locks—with a whisper,
Set ope the doors O soul.

Tenderly—be not impatient,
(Strong is your hold O mortal flesh,
Strong is your hold O love.)

Walt Whitman, "The Last Invocation"

FOR A LONG TIME Scott and I had both been interested in the subject of life after death. We had an intellectual curiosity about dying, great expectations of what it would be like, and now that Scott was coming closer to the end of his life we devoted much time to talking and reading about the subject. There were dozens of books on death and dying in our library, some of which (notably a rare three-volume set, *Before Death*, *At Death*, and *After Death* by the French astronomer Camille Flammarion) had belonged to my father years ago.

We believed in the continuity of life and continuance of consciousness in some form. We were eager for more encounters that we believed awaited us, more opportunities. Death, we felt, was a transition, not a termination. It was an exit-entrance between two areas of life.

In answer to a question on the subject from an old agnostic friend, Roger Baldwin, Scott wrote: "By many people death is considered an end. For others of us, death is a change; a good deal like the change from day to night—always thus far followed by another day. Never the same twice, but a procession of days.

"The human body turns into dust when the life force is withdrawn, only to be replaced by other forms that the life force assumes. The change, called death, is terminal for our bodies but not for higher expressions of the same life forces.

"I believe there is a revival, or survival, in some form. Our life goes on."

Scott had long talked of a purposeful and deliberate death. He was not going to wait until he was totally incapacitated and had become a burden to himself and others. He did not want to go through the horrors of a long decay in a nursing home.

"Why do we make such a hullaballoo of our last days and of dying?" he queried. Instead of quiet harmonious fading away in congenial familiar surroundings, we ship our loved ones to hospitals or nursing homes where, at great expense, they are maintained by strangers who try to stave off death by artificial means instead of easing and abetting the process. We enter with discomfort and a cry, but we can depart in dignity and completion, having fulfilled at least in part our purpose.

It almost seemed as though death had always been a part of our lives—what we had been working toward. The date and where we died were not important but the fact and how we faced it were of moment. We knew it would come and we looked forward to it. Scott, as A. S. M. Hutchinson wrote of a character in his 1925 novel *One Increasing Purpose*, "had the look of a man who stands at evening in his doorway, the day's work done, wide space before him; within, his house in order."

Scott wanted to go before his powers began to fail too far. He wanted to go of his own free will and accord, consciously and intentionally—a death by choice, cooperating with the process. He wanted no suppression of the death experience. He looked forward to learning and practicing the techniques of casting off the body voluntarily and easily. He would complete himself in death. He had learned how to live—now, how to die. Lao Tzu said: "Let life ripen and then let it fall." Scott's life had come to full ripeness; he was ready to let it go.

Dylan Thomas poesied: "Do not go gentle into that good night," but Scott desired his death to be gentle and reposeful as well as purposeful. He did not want to miss the ultimate experience; he did not want to muddle through or be unconscious. He wished to savor, even enjoy it. He particularly liked two accounts of serene deathbed scenes: one of Henry David Thoreau, the other of H. G. Wells.

In May 1862, Thoreau's sister wrote an account to a friend: "During his long illness I never heard a murmur escape from him or the slightest wish expressed to remain with us. His perfect contentment was truly wonderful, so full of life and good cheer did he seem. . . . His breathing grew fainter and fainter, and without the slightest struggle he left us." H. G. Wells was exceedingly inattentive when a reporter came to interview him during his last days. "Don't disturb me. Can't you see I'm busy dying?" were the only words the interviewer got. These two stories pleased Scott and doubtless gave him good examples for his own leave-taking.

How many ways are there to face and encounter death? As many as there are people dying. What it is like in reality we won't know until we go over ourselves, but we can make it a wrenching parting, a slammed door—or a harmonious climax, the crest. The key to our attitude and actions is in our hands. It would be good to go with open eyes and senses, to welcome the transition. If we prepare properly, we can sanely and serenely walk down the garden path, open the gate, and walk through, observing every step of the way. We all passed through birth—a far more dangerous and disruptive process—and survived. Now let's see what lies ahead.

Before Scott reached eighty, I had been outraged when he was called "an old man," though I allowed it after ninety. He had physical and mental and spiritual strength until his mid-nineties. Only then did he show dimunition of any of these qualities. Not even he, with his remarkable health, could escape old age. His heredity, his environment, his diet, his habits, his emotions, his mode of living—all had tended to keep him well until the inevitable ending.

He finished his last book, *Civilization and Beyond*, when he was ninety-two. Six publishers refused this depiction of what lies ahead on the ground that "it would not sell." Scott hired a printer to set it in type because he believed it gave an authentic survey of the dangerous course ahead for Western humanity and its grab-and-get culture. The book was published in 1975. He was working on a new book called *Social Forces* as late as 1982, a year before he died. We had made plans for more books together: one called *We Practice Health* (instead of practicing medicine) and, as an alternative to the "have more, get more" creed of modern life, a book called *Have Less, Be More*.

When Scott was ninety-six, I recognized and acknowledged his diminishing energies. His magnificent constitution was finally waning and his body wearing out. It was a worn-out implement and he was ready to set it aside and go on to what he hoped would be new and even more productive experiences. Freud wrote before his death, to a friend: "I am as weary as it is natural to be after a hardworking life, and I think I have fairly earned my rest. The organic elements that have held together for so long are tending to fall apart. Who would wish them to remain forcibly connected any longer?"

Past ninety-six, quoting Montaigne, Scott said: "I would like death to find me planting cabbages." He still worked in the garden and on the woodpile, though not with his former staying power. He was obviously no longer so compulsively active nor so strong, although he still chanted "Do your daily chores and bring the wood in from outdoors" as he carried in three logs instead of six, then finally, apologetically, one or two at a time.

He would recite with chagrin Oliver Wendell Holmes verse, "The Last Leaf":

. . .

They say that in his prime,
Ere the pruning knife of Time
Cut him down,
Not a better man was found
By the crier on his round
Through the town.

. . .

My grandmamma has said—
Poor old lady, she is dead
Long ago—
That he had a Roman nose
And his cheek was like a rose
In the snow;

But now his nose is thin,
And it rests upon his chin
Like a staff,
And a crook is in his back,
And a melancholy crack
In his laugh.

. . .

And if I should live to be
The last leaf upon the tree
    In the spring,
Let them smile, as I do now,
At the old forsaken bough
    Where I cling.

He quoted with amusement and nostalgia W. B. Yeats: " An aged man is but a paltry thing, a tattered coat upon a stick . . . fastened to a dying animal. . . ." And, What shall I do with this absurdity—O heart, / O troubled heart—this caricature, / Decrepit age that has been tied to me / As to a dog's tail?"

Out last trip abroad together was in 1980 when we went to India for an International Vegetarian Conference. On our return to the Untied States we flew to Iowa where at the State University, and later that month at Bowdoin College in Maine, Scott gave two of the best talks of this life. A comment came from one listener:" With the power and inner glow that Scott displayed at ninety-eight, I can only wonder what his oratorical skills must have been in his prime." Returning to Maine, we continued to grow our own food and cut our wood, to write and to welcome countless people.

Simone de Beauvoir wrote in *The Coming of Age*: "The greatest good fortune for the old person, even greater than health, is to have his world inhabited by projects; then, busy and useful, he escapes from boredom and from decay." Scott, at no point in his life, young or old, was ever bored or at a loss for interesting projects. "There is only one solution if old age is not to be an absurd parody of our former life, and that is to go on," said de Beauvoir, "pursuing ends that give our existence a meaning—devotion to individuals, to groups or to causes, social, political, intellectual or creative work."

Further on in her book de Beauvoir discusses a twenty-year scientific research project on people more than a hundred years old: "Most of the people in this group make careful plans for the future; they are interested in public affairs and are capable of youthful enthusiasm. They have their little fads and a sharp sense of humor; their appetites are good and they have great powers of resistance. They usually enjoy perfect mental health; they are optimistic and they show no sign of being afraid of death. . . . those people who . . . are more than a hundred years old are almost always quite exceptional beings."

Victor Hugo wrote in 1880, "For half a century I have been writing thoughts in prose, verse, history, drama, romance, tradition, satire, ode and song—I have tried them all; but I feel I have not said the thousandth part of that which is within me. When I go down to the grave, I can say 'I have finished my day's work,' but I cannot say 'I have finished my life's work.' My day's work will begin the next morning. The tomb is not a blind alley, it is an open thoroughfare; it closes in the twilight to open in the dawn. My work is only a beginning. It is hardly above its foundation. I would gladly see it mounting forever. The thirst for the Infinite proves infinity."

In a youth-oriented culture old age is underrated and derided. The quality that can manifest in old age is often ignored or disregarded. There can be perception, knowledge, wisdom, and good humor in old age that never was in youth. Like Adam in *As You Like It*, Scott's age was "as a lusty winter, frosty but kindly." With goals and motivation stretching ahead, old age for him was a time of fulfillment. Scott kept his strength and bearing all through his last decades: his seventies were not elderly, his eighties not decrepit, his nineties not senile. His mind was still alert, accurate, and keen in his late eighties, when he lectured as well as ever and read and wrote daily.

"Work," Scott said, "helps prevent one from getting old.

My work is my life. I cannot think of one without the other. The man who works and is never bored, is never old. A person is not old until regrets take the place of hopes and plans. Work and interest in worthwhile things are the best remedy for aging."

Still, he was facing the end. Interviewed in 1981 at age ninety-eight he said, "I look forward to the possibility of living until I'm ninety-nine." His blue eyes twinkled. "It is a precarious outlook, I assure you. With age your facility of expression and perception diminishes. I have almost nothing left but time. But if I can be of service, I would like to go on living."

Walt Whitman said at a far earlier age (seventy): "The old ship is not in a state to make many voyages, but the flag is still at the mast and I am still at the wheel." Of Mark Twain it was said: "He had produced his share of work in the world; he had outlived most of the people he cared for; the world was in a bad way and he was not averse to leaving it." A poet friend of Scott's, Richard Aldridge, wrote: "Not many left to talk to now. Not even much one wants to say. The day when he will not be here is not a very distant day."

I found in Scott's files a notation, carefully inscribed by hand on a three-by-five card: "As the personal ties that hold one to life weaken, that phase of life vanishes. The social side grows dimmer. The hold of the individual on life is correspondingly diminished."

Our evening hours after supper still provided time for serious reading. I found two paragraphs from a speech by Bhagwan Shree Rajneesh which I read to Scott: "The greatest mystery in life is not life itself, but death. Death is the culmination of life, the ultimate blossoming of life. In death the whole of life is summed up; in death you arrive. Life is a pilgrimage toward death. From the very beginning, death is coming. From the moment of birth, death has started coming towards you; you have started moving towards death. . . . And death is happening each moment in millions of ways all around the world. Existence lives through death; existence renews itself through death. Death is the greatest mystery—more mysterious than life, because life is only a pilgrimage toward death."

I read to him also from *The Egyptian Book of the Dead*:

Death is before me today, like the recovery of a sick man, like going forth into a garden after sickness.

Death is before me today, as a man longs to see his house after he has spent many years in captivity.

Death is before me today, like a physician with healing ointment for a man weary with shield- and sword-work.

I came across a profound paragraph in a 1913 book, *The Great Mother*, by C. H. Bjerregaard. "Turn which way we will, we find no 'killing principle' in Nature, only a vitalizing and sustaining one. Throughout its extent, Nature is life, in all forms and modifications—one vast and infinite life, subject no doubt to the extinction of particular phenomena, but never to absolute and total Death, even in its weakest and least of things. Anything that looks like Death is a token and certificate of life being about to start anew. Death and life are but the struggle of life itself to attain a higher form."

Another 1913 book, *Our Eternity* by Maurice Maeterlinck, yields this exalted passage: "Here begins the open sea. Here begins the glorious adventure, the only one abreast with human curiosity, the only one that soars as high as its highest longing. Let us accustom ourselves to regard death as a form of life which we do not yet understand; let us learn to look upon it with the same eye that looks upon birth; and soon our mind will be accompanied to the steps of the tomb with the same glad expectation as greets a birth."

Birth and death are but words that we've invented to express the limit of our knowledge. A friend wrote to us on the death of her own mother: "Death is only a horizon; and a horizon is nothing save the limit of our sight." I felt that Scott would merely go on ahead, ever seeking new horizons, and I was reminded of one of his favorite fables: "I am standing on the seashore. A ship at my side spreads her white sails to the morning breeze and starts for the blue ocean. She is an object of beauty and strength. I stand and watch her until at length she is only a ribbon of white cloud just where the sea and sky come to mingle with each other. There! She's gone! But someone at my side says, 'Gone where?' From our sight, that's all. She is just as large in mast and hull and spar as she was when she left our side; and just as able to bear her load of living freight to the place of destination. Her diminished size is in us, not in her. Just at the moment when you say, 'There! She's gone!' other voices are ready to take up the glad shout: 'There she comes!' And that is what we call dying."

Scott and I were winding up our lives together and we knew it. There were the physiological factors to be considered: how did he want to be treated, where, and by whom. I knew he desired to stay at home, not in a hospital with lifesaving apparatus all around. He would take no pills, no drugs, and hoped to avoid doctors. He had become less and less concerned with continuing to inhabit a weakening body. When he could no longer carry his part of the load and take care of himself, he was ready to go on. I was at one with him in this. The way one dies, it seemed to me, should reflect the way one had lived, and I was glad to help him do it gracefully.

In contemplating the approaching end I thought of the great lovings and leavings in my own life up to that point. Two shining moments stood out in my mind.

When my father was dying in a Florida hospital, my mother and I entered his room together. He was awake and looked up at us as we stood in the doorway. "My two favorite people," he whispered happily. It caused a lasting glow in both of us.

A rare thrill was given me by Scott in one word while he was being interviewed at home in Maine during his last year. He was asked to name the contemporary person who most influenced his life, apart from his heroes Tolstoy and Gandhi. He pondered the question, and after due reflection, he replied, "Helen." "With a young girl's cry of happiness," wrote the interviewer, "she rushed across the room to hug and kiss him for that ultimate tribute. He smiled into her face with wonderful sweetness."

With Scott slowing down, as invitations to speak came in, I filled the engagements and he stayed quietly at home. One of the last letters he wrote by hand was sent to the Community Church of Boston:

> Friends:
>
> For about a year I have been getting older rather rapidly. One day I feel in good health. The next day may be an off day. Under these conditions I cannot bind myself to talk on any specific date. Too bad! But such is life. Until this year I was fairly sure of myself. Now I cannot even be sure for the immediate future. Under these circumstances I should not take on formal speaking engagements. Wishing you a good season . . .

It was a new stage in our relationship and not a welcome one for me, but I would do what I could to cope with the emergency. I arranged for friends to watch over him when I had to be away. Here is a list of specifics I left as instructions, indicating the daily tasks and his condition:

Make fire in kitchen.

Feed fire in living room.

Let Scott sleep as long as possible.

Sit in kitchen or living room until he wakes.

Help him into outer shirts or sweaters.

Straighten up blankets on his couch but leave them there during the day.

Make tea when water boils on the wood stove and give him a glass of juice and a banana. That's all he gets till lunch, unless he wants some popcorn.

He'll want to get wood and work outdoors most of the morning if the weather is good.

He gets soup and some wheat or kasha at noon for lunch, with an apple or banana, peanut butter and honey.

He should have his nap on his couch before or after lunch.

Around 1:30 you might get the mail and read it, then put it in the big empty box in his downstairs room for me.

He'll want to be out during the afternoon if the weather is good.

At four o'clock kick up the kitchen fire.

Put on baking potatoes or beets or rutabagas or carrots.

At 5:30 I make a salad; we eat at six usually.

He goes to bed around 8:30; you can sit and read!

A year or two after moving to Maine, we had both paid our dues in a funerary society and arranged for our own cremations in advance. All I had to do at this time was to follow Scott's instructions which he left me as a "Memorandum to Whom It May Concern," written in 1963 and initialed in 1968 and again in 1982.

This memorandum is written in order to place on record the following requests:

1. When it comes to my last illness I wish the death process to follow its natural course; consequently:
   a. I wish to be at home—not in a hospital.
   b. I prefer that no doctor should officiate. The medics seem to know little about life, and next to nothing about death.
   c. If at all possible, I wish to be outside near the end; in the open, not under a roof.
   d. I wish to die fasting; therefore, as death approaches I would prefer to abstain from food and, if possible, likewise from liquids.

2. I wish to be keenly aware of the death process; therefore, no sedatives, painkillers, or anaesthetics.

3. I wish to go quickly and as quietly as possible. Therefore:
   a. No injections, heart stimulants, forced feeding, no oxygen, and especially no blood transfusions.
   b. No expressions of regret or sorrow, but rather, in the hearts and actions of those who may be present, calmness, dignity, understanding, joy, and peaceful sharing of the death experience.
   c. Manifestation is a vast field of experience. As I have lived eagerly and fully, to the extent of my powers, so I pass on gladly and hopefully. Death is either a transition or an awakening. In either case it is to be welcomed, like every other aspect of the life process.

4. The funeral and other incidental details.
   a. Unless the law requires, I direct that no undertaker, mortician, or other professional manipulator of corpses be consulted, be called in, or participate in any way in the disposal of my body.
   b. I direct that as soon as convenient after my death my friends place my body in a plain wooden box made of spruce or pine boards; the body to be dressed in working clothes, and

to be laid on my sleeping bag. There is to be no ornament or decoration of any kind in or on the box.

c. The body so dressed and laid out to be taken to the Auburn, Maine crematorium of which I am a paid member, and there cremated privately.

d. No funeral services are to be held. Under no circumstances is any preacher, priest, or other professional religionist to officiate at any time or in any way between death and the disposal of the ashes.

e. As soon as convenient after cremation, I request my wife, Helen K. Nearing, or if she predecease me or not be able to, some other friend to take the ashes and scatter them under some tree on our property facing Spirit Cove.

5. I make all these requests in full consciousness and the hope that they will be respected by those nearest to me who may survive me.

I worked out a leaflet of around thirty telling quotations on death, had it printed and ready to send to friends when he died, needing only to fill in the final date. It was seen and approved by Scott in the year before he went. Here are some excerpts:

> Thou hast embarked,
> Thou hast made the voyage,
> Thou art come to shore.
> Get out.
>
> Marcus Aurelius, *Meditations*, A.D. 160

When the seed bursts, the plant then suddenly spreads asunder. At that instant it feels that it is being dissolved, after lying so long narrowly folded in the seed. On the contrary it gains a new world. . . . Birth must seem to the new-born babe what death seems to us—the annihilation of all the conditions which had hitherto made life possible in the womb of its mother, but proved to be its emergence into a wider life.

> Gustave Fechner, *Life After Death*, 1836

Nobody knows that death stays the development of the individual. It stays our perception of it, but so does distance, absence, or even sleep. Birth gave to each of us much; death may give much more, in the way of subtler senses to behold colours we cannot here see, to catch sounds we do not now hear, and to be aware of bodies and objects impalpable at present to us.

Sir Edwin Arnold, Death and Afterwards, 1901

Who that has mourned and not failed of the promised comfort can ever question the living fact of immortality? Has the body a soul? No. The soul has a body. And well does that soul know when this body has served its purpose, and well does that soul do to lay it aside in high austerity, taking it off like a stained garment.

Lucien Price, Litany for All Souls, 1924

We cannot suppose that death is the end of any adventure except that of the body. . . . There will be things yet to be done, and the stuff that we work in will be the utterly familiar and still mysterious and exciting stuff of ourselves.

Mary Austin, Experiences Facing Death, 1931

The last months of his life, lying quietly on his couch, Scott would speak aloud as if to himself or to someone unseen, and he would talk in his sleep as if in conversation. I took down what I could of it.

"I slept so sound. I was almost gone. I have been told that the probabilities are that I can be released if I want. I'm free to come or go. It's partly up to me to decide. I want to stay as long as I'm wanted. . . . "

"I should be making the fires. Is there snow around the house? Should I bring more books in?"

"It's been wonderful with you. You've been a very nice companion, lovey. Very loving. It's certainly been a good life.

Couldn't have been better. It's been good, good. . . . Wonderful to be with you. Love and marriage. Yes, marriage . . . "

"You did a good job in finishing the house. It does not require much upkeep. It works very well. A good name for it: The Good Life Center. It will be better than I imagined."

One night, while asleep, he seemed to be pondering outloud. "The human race is on trial. They've been given their chance, plenty of chances, and they've done a second-rate job. There are so many of them now and they're so ineffective. Weighed in the balance and found wanting. The repentance and regeneration has got to come from within, and where is it? Maybe we should be got rid of with the least suffering and trouble."

Another night he had a dream in which he was one of a group to draw up a world constitution to prepare people for the next step in human evolution. "We must accept the amount of discipline necessary to take this next step. A cheerful acceptance of the discipline necessary to enable us to undergo training for the next step forward in fulfilling our appointed tasks. Everyone is not capable of the necessary motivation and self-discipline. This is not freedom; this is participation in joint activity, not freedom but coordinated purpose. Freedom does not enable one to do any of the essential work of the universe."

In his sleep one night he uttered a question, "Can mankind function productively, creatively, dependably?" and seemed to listen to an answer.

He told me of a vision he had one evening. "I was in the valley for the first time. I never had the sense of it before. I didn't expect to see it so large, historically and culturally. I don't think we have any words to describe it. It's the difference between air and water. [Smiling beatifically] Hail to Light and Beauty! [Saying his name] Nearing. Yes, he kept careful records. In every sense he was a scientific man. Is that what you had in mind for him to be? [Smiling] I heard most of that, yes. In other words, another life. It began a long time ago . . . Hope to return soon—much better prepared."

A friend and neighbor asked him toward the end: "What are you thinking these days?"

After a pause he answered: "It is a rare opportunity to have lived so long and to have experienced so much—and particularly advantageously located to speak out. We, Helen and I, have been together for half a century. Have had a unique position together—to have worked as a team.

"I am particularly concerned with society. The particular social pattern we call Western civilization is progressively breaking up. Is there a future for it? After a hundred years in it I can speak with a certain amount of authority. I am profoundly concerned that the human race does its job thoroughly and persistently till it is complete.

"What is its job? The earth is a speck of dust in an enormous expression of life; one grain of consciousness in the totality. The human role in this drama has been more or less thoroughly muffed. We are fumbling with the ball. We have frittered away our time. Can we hold together and remake and rebuild something more worthwhile? I would like to make my contribution toward producing and creating a better world. This is what we are here to do.

"It is that which occupies my mind these last days of my life."

I took down on tape recorder this conversation two months before he died. "My purpose? My purpose is to live the kind of life that will mean the most to you, to me, to the universe immediately around us, and to some part of the universe that lies a little beyond what we see around us.

"In other words, I may be at the portal of a doorway, of looking at least into another type of being, another type of existence, another type of experience."

"You welcome that?" I asked.

"I have no choice. It's like asking if I expect the sun to rise tomorrow. The life people have been living is so far away from the real purpose. We've got to stop fooling around and move toward a new way of life.

"Do the thing that you believe in. Do the best you can in the place where you are and be kind.

"I'd like to get people into the habit of living physically and mentally in such a way that when they get all through, the earth could be a better place to live in than it was.

"Sit back and be comfortable? That's no way to be. Sit up. Move forward. Keep going. I'd like to get out and plant potatoes; cut wood, anything constructive.

"I would like to live as long as I'm useful. If I can be of use, I would like to go on living. If I can't even carry in the wood for you, I might as well go."

He might have quoted the words of the ailing king of France in *All's Well That Ends Well*: "'Let me not live,' quoth he, / 'After my flame lacks oil,' . . . Since I nor wax nor honey can bring home, / I quickly were dissolvèd from my hive / To give some laborers room."

A month and a half before Scott went, a month before his hundredth birthday, while sitting with a group at the table one day, he said: "I think I won't eat any more." He never took solid food again. He deliberately and purposefully chose the time and the way of his leaving. It was to be methodical and conscious. He would cast off his body by fasting.

Death by fasting is not a violent form of suicide; it is a slow gentle dimunition of energies, a peaceful way to leave, voluntarily. Externally and internally he was prepared. He had always liked Robert Louis Stevenson's "Glad did I live and gladly die, and I lay me down with a will." Now he could put this into practice. He himself inaugurated his own technique for dying: let the body itself give up its life.

I acquiesced, realizing how animals often leave life—creeping away out of sight and denying themselves food. For a month I fed Scott just on juices when he wanted any liquids: apple, orange, banana, grape, whatever he could swallow. Then he said: "I would like only water." Yet he did not sicken. He was still lucid and spoke with me, but his body was extremely emaciated. The life force in him was lessening.

A week more on water, and he was completely detached from life, ready to slip easily into that good night. His body had dried up; now it was withering away, and he could tranquilly and peacefully retire from it. I was with him on his couch and quietly urged him on, the morning of August 24, 1983.

Half aloud, I intoned an old Native American chant: "Walk tall as the trees; live strong as the mountains; be gentle as the spring winds; keep the warmth of summer in your heart, and the Great Spirit will always be with you."

"You don't have to hold on to anything, my love," I murmured to him. "Just let go of the body. Go with the tide. Flow with it. You have lived a fine life. You have done your bit. Enter into a new life. Go into the light. Love goes with you. Everything here is all right."

Slowly, gradually, he detached himself, breathing less and less, fainter and fainter; then he was off and free, like a dry leaf from the tree, floating down and away. "All . . . right," he breathed, seeming to testify to the all-rightness of everything, and was gone. I felt the visible pass into the invisible.

Our love affair had lasted half a century and still goes on now, eight years after he died at the honorable age of one hundred. The love continues on my part, and on his side, too, I believe. From where else could come the glad certainty every morning, evening, and hour of the day that I live in love and am charged with it—outgoing and incoming. Since the day Scott died, I have had a sense of his continued being. As Winnenap the Shoshone medicine man said: "If the dead be truly dead, why should they still be walking in my heart?" Scott remains a large part of my life—a permanent presence.

Krishnamurti, in one of his later books, wrote "There can be no lasting happiness in relationships." I found a lasting happiness in my relationship with Scott even after his death. I believe in love after death as well as in life after death.

[I will go to third person for a while.]

Scott lived the good life and died the good death. He had lived fully at every moment and he died serenely. He went as he had wished—at home, without medications, doctors, or hospital confinement, and with Helen beside him. She had a joyous feeling that he had done well. Leonardo da Vinci wrote in 1500: "As a well-spent day brings happy sleep, so life well-used brings happy death."

There was no disturbance; he did not gasp or jerk or tremble. He just breathed softly until there was no breath left and he was no longer in the body. It was simple as could be. It was an easy passing and a beautiful one, just breathing life away.

Having aided and abetted the planned departure, without grief she witnessed his ending. She felt his deliverance more than her own loss. She was happy for him to go thus, and resolved to do the same in her own good time. A few more years were left to her to round out her life and contribute what she could before taking her own departure. Scott's dying showed her how to do it when her time came. She felt that it was the love that mattered, not the personality that was passing. The essence, the substance of his being, remained in existence. The covering, the husk, was necessarily ephemeral.

Two writings sustained her, then and now. One by Patience Worth from *The Sorry Tale*, a 1910 book:

> The eyes be hid, what care ye?
> The hands be not, what care ye?
> The love hath stepped from earth—
> What think ye love shall lose?
> Heart that stoppeth beating ne'er stoppeth love.

And one from the heroine of Thomas Hardy's *The Wood-landers*:

> Whenever I get up I'll think of 'ee, and whenever I lie down I'll think of 'ee. Whenever I plant the young larches I'll think that none can plant as you planted; and whenever I spit a gad, and whenever I turn the cider-wring I'll say none could do it like you. If ever I forget your name, let me forget home and heaven. But no, my love, I never could forget 'ee; for you was a good man and did good things.

Scott had wished no funeral or memorial services to be held after his death, but many in the neighboring towns wished for some gathering to honor him. So a Celebration of his Life was held two weeks after his death, at the Blue Hill town hall, some twenty miles away from Harborside. There was music, flute playing, and a record of Kathleen Ferrier singing a Brahms song; Helen read one of his favorite stories, "The Hunter," from Olive Schreiner's *Dreams*; and neighbors stood up as in Quaker meeting and testified to what Scott had brought to their lives. It turned out to be a happy celebration as she had hoped.

[Back to "me" and "we."]

Though this was the ending of a significant chapter in my life, I felt that even in his leaving Scott had taught me. I had witnessed in his benign going a natural death, when the act of living had actually spent itself of its own momentum. He had taken his time; he had gone when he wished. His death had illuminated his life.

I looked forward to my own death—in a kind of rapture, seeing death of the body as a release from physical life. I wanted to slip off, to loose the moorings, to pass on into the unknown, to be one with the All, no longer a separate, consequential being. I craved elimination of the sensational bodyness. Death might prove to be a great, final, endless meditation. I have discarded notions of what it is supposed to be and am ready for what will happen or not happen.

British writer Malcolm Muggeridge wrote in "What I Believe": "As for death, if there is nothing beyond, then for the nothingness I offer thanks; if another mode of existence, with this old worn-out husk of a body left behind, this floundering, muddled mind given a longer range and a new precision, then for that likewise I offer thanks." I feel also a great gratitude for life, and a great gratitude that death can end it beautifully.

We don't have to go on living bedridden, ailing, and incapacitated. We don't have to go through the horror of a long decay in a nursing home. If we are at home and have made our wishes known, we can stop eating. It is as simple as that. Eliminate nurses and food, and death stands welcome before us.

Scott's dying showed me the good way, the good death—a negation of pain and distress, with the currents of life still flowing on. For such there is no grief. In the loss of something there was the gain of something else: a glimpse of hope in this reposeful, purposeful ending.

There is a curtain between our lives and deaths. Should it be lifted? Should not one world be tackled at a time? I had already more than dabbled in spiritualism. I had ventured with communication in séances, had channeled as a medium long before the Shirley MacLaines and hundreds of others now doing it were born. I had done automatic writing, worked Ouija boards, and so on. I had tried them all, with worthwhile and even stimulating promptings and messages from "over there."

But, curiously enough, I tried none of these openings after Scott died. I did not want to detain him in his further search for truth. He was finished with the earth plane; let him not be concerned with the life he had left. He was tuned into different fields, another frequency. He should not be expected to lower his to mine, and I was not yet accomplished enough to raise mine to his. We were operating from different stations for the time being.

So I have no recollection of psychic contact with Scott after his death. But there is a welling up of love for him which I have felt through the years he has been gone whenever I think of him, which is often often.

As William James wrote in "Confidences of a Psychical Researcher," "I confess that at times I have been tempted to believe that the creator has eternally intended this department of nature to remain *baffling*, to prompt our curiosities and hopes and suspicions all in equal measure, so that although ghosts, and clairvoyances, and raps and messages from spirits, are always seeming to exist and can never be fully explained away, they also can never be susceptible of full corroboration."

Scott's hundredth birthday, August 6, and his death day, August 24, were less than three weeks apart. For both days tributes in the way of cards and letters and cables poured in upon us. There were finally over a thousand—congratulations and then condolences. Half of them were from people he had never met but who were affected by his books and lectures or by his reputation. There were officially typed letters of esteem, and there were handwritten scrawls of praise and appreciation such as: "You have served truth, and you have served justice even when it was denied you. Above all you have respected the dignity of work more than anyone I know."

All thanked him for the influence he had had on their lives and thinking. All were noteworthy and touching, perhaps none more than two postcards, one from an unknown man who drew a figure with an upraised axe over a block of wood and merely the words "Goodbye, Scott," and a poetic postcard handwritten by our local mail carrier: "Scott will be remembered as a man who gave forth knowledge, a way of life, and a new line of thinking. When the word is received that Nature has called another, we shall listen, and pause—then go on our way, knowing full well that here was a man who altered and improved the direction of many."

There were letters from the butcher's union (to a vegetarian!), from unknown professors who had been inspired by his example, from the president of the University of Pennsylvania (the alma mater that ousted him), and of course from hundreds of friends and acquaintances.

One man wrote: "It was a great day when you turned your back on what is represented by the Wharton School and went into the wilderness. Albert Schweitzer did the same thing in 1913. At that time he was the intellectual darling of Europe. As it turned out, his fame as a servant humanitarian catapulted him into greater fame than the warring continent could ever best. You must know by now that your metamorphosis has very much turned out the same way."

The first winter that Scott was no longer on the scene I spent answering by hand the more than one thousand messages and letters and cards that had come in. I have preserved them in twelve large scrapbooks which will be given with his other papers to Boston University's Mugar Memorial Library and to the Peace Collection at Swarthmore College in Pennsylvania. Meanwhile they are kept at Forest Farm for all to see.

For me, there followed some productive years. I had yearnings to settle permanently in Holland, my mother's homeland and the place of my early adult years, but obligations with the Good Life Center kept me at home. I wanted to write another book, this one, primarily about Scott. I would like the world to know him as he was himself, and to share his peaceful intentional and predetermined ending. His was a life so well lived that I knew at whatever point I dipped into it I would bring up light: as Graham Balfour wrote of Robert Louis Stevenson, "to dig into the past of a dead friend, and find him, at every spadeful, shine brighter."

When I reached eighty-five, six years after Scott's death, I suddenly found myself in old age. As Trotsky wrote in *Diary in Exile*: "Old age is one of the most unexpected of all things that happen to one."

In the spring of the previous year I had bicycled easily through northern Holland with a group of elder citizens. I went on to Greece to help conduct a workshop there. I was invited to a women's conference in Moscow. How long could I continue at that pace? There was vigor, but not the same surety in my body: no more leaping from rock to rock. I now knew how Scott must have felt, although for him it came in his nineties, with fears of falling, a confusion of memory over paperwork, finances, and figures—disagreeable matters to face.

I had been pedaling for a long time in high gear. Now I realized I was coasting, decidedly going downhill, no longer able to climb energetically as I had previously so easily done. There was now a sense of letting go, of slowing down. The job, such as it had been, was almost done. I had been a carefree and happy traveler; now I was on the homestretch, the end was just around the bend.

Life without death would be unbearable. Physical life forever? Death and corruption all around one: relationships strained and tangled; one's son's son's sons and one's great-great-great-grandfathers all surviving and mixed up with one's great-grandfathers and great-great-grandfathers?!

Death eases us off after a decent interval of so many score years. It is the end of the day; one is let out of school, handed one's walking papers, and told to take a rest. It is over for now. Death is a vacation out of physical life, a new turning point. We couldn't get along without it; we should welcome it. When the day's work is ended, night brings the benison of sleep; death can be the beginning of a larger day.

It became fascinating to me to observe, to watch, to tabulate the possible years, days, moments of survival still ahead. I was finally experiencing old age and finding it not without compensations. One can savor sights and sounds more deeply when one gets really old. It may be the last time you see a sunset, a tree, the snow, or know winter. The sea, a lake, all become as in childhood, magical and a great wonder: then seen for the first time, now perhaps for the last. Music, bird songs, the wind, the waves: one listens to tones with deeper delight and appreciation—"loving well," to borrow from Shakespeare's seventy-third sonnet, "that which I must leave ere long."

All is evanescent, fleeting. Will one be there to hear and see tomorrow—to catch the glow of the sun sinking behind the hills, to hear the first birdcall, to sense the deep silence of a midnight sky? If not, let's taste it deeply now, take it into our being, chew and absorb it.

There was for me a rendering up of responsibilities and a relief to be soon done with dates, calendars, and contacts. It was something new for me to feel so detached—no need of the world, nor did the world need me—although two of my favorite authors, Robert Louis Stevenson and Richard Bach, would dispute this. They pointed to further efforts before departing the earth scene. Stevenson wrote engagingly in his *Crabbed Age and Youth* about it being decidedly harder to climb trees and not nearly so hard to sit still, yet "if we are indeed here to perfect and complete our own natures and grow larger, stronger for some nobler career in the future, we had all best bestir ourselves to the utmost while we have the time." And Richard Bach gives a test in his *Reluctant Messiah* "to find whether your mission on earth is finished: if you're still alive, it isn't." Reconsidering, I would agree with them.

I wrote a personal summation for myself of what Scott meant to me.

I have lived beside several great people, none I came to love and honor more than Scott Nearing. Every detail of his life with me was in harmony with the high ideals he professed. He was in tune with his universe. He was a man who tried to live what he believed, who practiced what he preached. I never knew anybody so true to himself and what he believed to be right, cost what it might to speak it out and to live it.

He was many-sided and full of opposite qualities. He was an idealist, but a tough practical worker—a *practical* idealist. He was essentially religious, but member of no church, adherent to no religious group; a man of letters, but a grubby gardener; a public figure, and a happy hermit; an orator of note, very vocal, but not a voluble talker in ordinary conversation. He was a person who didn't understand or particularly appreciate music, but always after me to practice and play my violin. He was a terse and factual writer on academic subjects, but with a chuckling sense of humor in daily life.

He was a great and generous soul. It was truly a good life to live for half a century with a man of his caliber. We shared a richness of experience and feeling that gave depth to our years of voluntary simplicity.

I composed a last letter to him, written after his death, to be put in the celestial mailbox.

Dearly Scott:

Fifty years we lived together in love and comradeship. Matrimony never seemed an essential part of it. We linked together as two persons whose interests and aims and actions coincided. We liked many things together, as well as liking each other. Your intellect and training were far above mine; your skills were more developed; your experience wider, yet we met and worked together on a plane of understanding and cooperation that lifted me beyond my scant abilities. We seemed equal in some subtle way and we lived our lives as one.

Thank you, and all the best to you forever.

Helen

Though all is constantly changing, nothing is lost in the universe. Everything is connected with everything else by the iron law of cause and effect. Perhaps there is only one sin—separateness—with the blessedness of love making all whole. I feel that life is such a unity that love which once happened still exists. It is there on the record. Love once felt has its place.

The love I had for and received from Scott, the love for and from countless women and men I have known, is still vibrating in the world. Everyone who feels "I love" adds to the heavenly glow. The love that has been felt all through the ages, everywhere, all through time . . . what a shining! What an eternal process and presence! Love is the source, love the goal, and love the method of attainment.

A network of love crisscrosses the globe. The delicate shining lines form a tenuous web from one end of the world to the other. There are so many threads of love in the world, so much love going on, for and from so many people. To have partaken of and to have given love is the greatest of life's rewards. There seems never an end to the loving that goes on forever and ever. Loving and leaving are a part of living.

Selected Bibliography

Books by Helen Nearing

1974   *The Good Life Album of Helen and Scott Nearing*. New York: E. P. Dutton.

1980   *Simple Food for the Good Life*. New York: Delta/ Eleanor Friede.

1980   *Wise Words on the Good Life*. New York: Schocken.

1983   *Our Home Made of Stone*. Camden, Maine: Down East Books.

Coauthored with Scott Nearing

1950   *The Maple Sugar Book*. New York: John Day.

1954   *Living the Good Life*. New York: Schocken.

1955   *USA Today*. Harborside, Maine: Social Science Institute (hereafter: SSI).

1958   *Socialists around the World*. Harborside, Maine: SSI.

1958   *The Brave New World*. Harborside, Maine: SSI.

1959   *Our Right to Travel*. Harborside, Maine: SSI.

1977   *Building and Using Our Sun-heated Greenhouse*. Charlotte, Vt.: Garden Way.

1979   *Continuing the Good Life*. New York: Schocken.

Books by Scott Nearing

1908   *Economics*. (with Frank D. Watson) New York: Macmillan.

1911   *Social Adjustment*. New York: Macmillan.
         The Solution of the Child Labor Problem. New York: Row Peterson.

1912   *The Super Race*. New York: Huebsch.
         Women and Social Progress. (with Nellie Seeds) New York: Macmillan.

1913   *Social Sanity*. New York: Row Peterson.
         Financing the Wage Earner's Family. New York: Row Peterson.

Selected Bibliography

Books by Helen Nearing

1974   *The Good Life Album of Helen and Scott Nearing.* New York: E. P. Dutton.

1980   *Simple Food for the Good Life.* New York: Delta/ Eleanor Friede.

1980   *Wise Words on the Good Life.* New York: Schocken.

1983   *Our Home Made of Stone.* Camden, Maine: Down East Books.

Coauthored with Scott Nearing

1950   *The Maple Sugar Book.* New York: John Day.

1954   *Living the Good Life.* New York: Schocken.

1955   *USA Today.* Harborside, Maine: Social Science Institute (hereafter: SSI).

1958   *Socialists around the World.* Harborside, Maine: SSI.

1958   *The Brave New World.* Harborside, Maine: SSI.

1959   *Our Right to Travel.* Harborside, Maine: SSI.

1977   *Building and Using Our Sun-heated Greenhouse.* Charlotte, Vt.: Garden Way.

1979   *Continuing the Good Life.* New York: Schocken.

Books by Scott Nearing

1908   *Economics.* (with Frank D. Watson) New York: Macmillan.

1911   *Social Adjustment.* New York: Macmillan.
       The Solution of the Child Labor Problem. New York: Row Peterson.

1912   *The Super Race.* New York: Huebsch.
       Women and Social Progress. (with Nellie Seeds) New York: Macmillan.

1913   *Social Sanity.* New York: Row Peterson.
       Financing the Wage Earner's Family. New York: Row Peterson.

1914   *Wages in the United States.* New York: Macmillan.
       Reducing the Cost of Living. Philadelphia: Jacob.
1915   *Income.* New York: Macmillan
       Anthracite. Philadelphia: Winston.
       The New Education. Philadelphia: Winston.
1916   *Social Religion.* New York: Macmillan.
       Poverty and Riches. Philadelphia: Winston Community.
       Civics. (with Jessie Field) Philadelphia: Winston.
       The Germs of War. St. Louis: National Rip-Saw.
1917   *The Great Madness.* New York: Rand School.
1918   *The Elements of Economics.* New York: Rand School.
1919   *The Trial of Scott Nearing.* New York: Rand School.
1921   *The American Empire.* New York: Rand School.
1922   *The Next Step.* New York: Social Science Publications.
1923   *Oil and the Germs of War.* Ridgewood, N.J.: the author.
1925   *Educational Frontiers.* New York: Seltzer.
       Dollar Diplomacy. (with Joseph Freeman) Philadelphia:
       Huebsch.
1926   *Education in Soviet Russia.* New York: International
       The British General Strike. New York: International.
1927   *Whither China?* New York: International.
       The Economic Organization of the Soviet Union. New York:
       Vanguard.
       Where is Civilization Going? New York: Vanguard.
1929   *Black America.* New York: Vanguard. Republished 1969,
       New York: Schocken.
1930   *The Twilight of Empire.* New York: Vanguard.
1931   *War.* New York: Vanguard.
1932   *Must We Starve?* New York: Vanguard.
       Free Born: An Unpublishable Novel. New York: Urquhart.
1933   *Fascism.* Jamaica, Vt.: the author.
1945   *United World.* New York: Island Press.
       The Soviet Union as a World Power. New York: Island Press.
       Democracy Is Not Enough. New York: Island Press.
       The Tragedy of Empire. New York: Island Press.
1946   *War or Peace?* New York: Island Press.
1947   *The Revolution of Our Time.* New York: Island Press.
1952   *Economics for the Power Age.* New York: John Day.

1954   *Man's Search for the Good Life.* Harborside, Maine: SSI.
1956   *To Promote the General Welfare.* Harborside, Maine: SSI.
1958   *Soviet Education.* Harborside, Maine: SSI.
1961   *Freedom: Promise and Menace.* Harborside, Maine: SSI.
1962   *Economic Crisis in the United States.* Harborside, Maine: SSI.
       Socialism in Practice. New York: New Century.
1963   *Cuba and Latin America.* Harborside, Maine: SSI.
1965   *The Conscience of a Radical.* Harborside, Maine: SSI.
1972   *The Making of a Radical.* New York: Harper/Colophon.
1975   *Civilization and Beyond.* Harborside, Maine: SSI.